Connections

Worship
Companion

ALSO AVAILABLE IN THIS SERIES

Connections Worship Companion, Year C, Volume 1
Connections Worship Companion, Year C, Volume 2
Connections Worship Companion, Year A, Volume 1
Connections Worship Companion, Year A, Volume 2

Year B, Volume 1

Advent through Pentecost

Connections

Worship
Companion

David Gambrell, editor

WESTMINSTER
JOHN KNOX PRESS
LOUISVILLE · KENTUCKY

© 2023 Westminster John Knox Press

First Edition
Published by Westminster John Knox Press
Louisville, Kentucky

23 24 25 26 27 28 29 30 31 32—10 9 8 7 6 5 4 3 2 1

Unless otherwise indicated, Scripture quotations are from the New Revised Standard Version of the Bible, copyright © 1989 by the Division of Christian Education of the National Council of the Churches of Christ in the U.S.A., and are used by permission. Scripture quotations from the NRSV have been adapted for inclusive language.

Permission is granted to churches to reprint individual prayers and liturgical texts for worship provided that the following notice is included: Reprinted by permission of Westminster John Knox Press from *Connections Worship Companion.* Copyright 2023.

Book design by Drew Stevens
Cover design by Allison Taylor

Library of Congress Cataloging-in-Publication Data

Names: Gambrell, David, editor.
Title: Connections worship companion : Year C / David Gambrell.
Description: First edition. | Louisville, Kentucky : Westminster John Knox
  Press, 2021. | Series: Connections: a lectionary commentary for
  preaching and worship | Includes index. | Summary: "Part of the
  Connections commentary series, these worship resources help
  congregations illuminate the connections between Scripture and
  liturgical rhythms. A "Making Connections" essay precedes each
  liturgical season's resources, providing context for worship within the
  themes and purpose of the season"-- Provided by publisher.
Identifiers: LCCN 2021023009 (print) | LCCN 2021023010 (ebook) | ISBN
  9780664264963 (hardback) | ISBN 9781646982080 (ebook)
Subjects: LCSH: Common lectionary (1992). Year C. | Public worship. |
  Worship programs.
Classification: LCC BV199.L42 C66 2021 (print) | LCC BV199.L42 (ebook) |
  DDC 264.05--dc23
LC record available at https://lccn.loc.gov/2021023009
LC ebook record available at https://lccn.loc.gov/2021023010

Connections Worship Companion, Year B, Volume 1
ISBN: 9780664264949 (hardback)
ISBN: 9781646983544 (ebook)

Most Westminster John Knox Press books are available at special quantity discounts when purchased in bulk by corporations, organizations, and special-interest groups. For more information, please e-mail SpecialSales@wjkbooks.com.

Contents

TIME AFTER THE EPIPHANY

SEASON OF LENT

SEASON OF EASTER

Supplements for the Narrative Lectionary

Introduction

This is not a book of prayers—
at least not yet.

These words will not become prayers
until the Holy Spirit breathes them,
until the body of Christ speaks and hears them,
until the people of God live them
in acts of service and love.

These words come from different people
in different places of ministry—
pastors and poets,
students and scholars,
activists and artists,
evangelists and educators,
bakers and baristas,
mission workers and musicians.

They have different voices,
and those voices will resonate
with different worshipers
in different ways.

It will be up to you,
as a planner and leader of worship,
to make these words sing:

to pray them
among the beloved people of God
with honesty, passion, wonder, and grace;

to enact them
as the whole body of Christ
with heart, mind, soul, and strength;

to transform them
through the gifts of the Spirit,
with rhythm, color, texture, and taste.

You are encouraged, then,
even challenged,
even required
to find your own voice,
to inhabit these texts,
to adapt them as needed,
so that these words
may become the prayers
of your people
in your place
for the sake of the world,
all people,
in every place.

Only then
will these words become prayers.

Only then
will they rise like incense before God,
joining the intercession
of our great high priest,
Christ Jesus,
who still teaches us to pray.

David Gambrell

How to Use This Book

Three kinds of materials are provided in this volume. First, at the beginning of each major section is a short essay titled "Making Connections." These brief passages of commentary have several purposes:

- they introduce the primary theological themes of a given time in the Christian year;
- they highlight a particular biblical text, drawn from the lectionary, that may be used as a kind of lens for magnifying and examining the themes of the season;
- they point to distinctive features of the lectionary cycle included in this volume; and

- they offer practical and pastoral guidance for leaders as they seek to prepare faithful, thoughtful, creative, and engaging worship for the people of God.

These essays can be used in discussion with worship committees, planning teams, or church staff groups to promote biblical study, inspire theological reflection, and inform liturgical action.

Second, each section includes a collection of seasonal/repeating resources. These are liturgical texts intended for use during a certain span of time in the Christian year, whether occasionally or for several weeks in a row. Specifically, these resources include the following acts of worship:

Confession and Pardon
Prayer for Illumination
Thanksgiving for Baptism
Great Thanksgiving
Prayer after Communion
Prayer of Thanksgiving (for the dedication of the offering when the
    Eucharist is not celebrated)
Blessing

These texts are somewhat broader and more general in their theological content and liturgical language, and they are designed for multiple uses within a liturgical season or period of Ordinary Time. They promote diachronic (meaning "through time") connections from one Sunday to the next, deriving their benefit from regular engagement with the church's tradition as people return to worship from week to week. They emphasize central convictions of Christian faith and life, supporting the kind of faith formation that takes place through sustained, long-term participation in worship. These texts are especially connected with the celebration of the sacraments.

Third, there is a set of resources for each Sunday or festival in the Christian year. Specifically, these resources include the following elements of the service:

Opening Sentences (or Call to Worship)
Prayer of the Day (or Gathering Prayer)
Invitation to Discipleship
Prayers of Intercession
Invitation to Offering
Invitation to the Table
Charge

These texts are somewhat narrower and more specific in their theological content and liturgical language, and they are designed for use on a given Sunday or festival in the Christian year. They promote synchronic (meaning "same time") connections between the liturgy and the lectionary, deriving their benefit from flashes of insight that collect around a common word, image, or phrase from the biblical texts for the day. They emphasize particular practices of Christian faith and life, supporting the kind of faith formation that takes place in more concentrated, short-term experiences of worship. These texts are especially connected with the proclamation of the word.

By combining the **seasonal/repeating resources (in bold type)** with the *Sunday/festival elements (in italics)*, as well as other elements not provided in this resource (in regular type), as indicated below, worship planners will be able to assemble complete orders of worship for the Lord's Day.

GATHERING

Opening Sentences
Hymn, Psalm, or Spiritual Song
Prayer of the Day
Confession and Pardon

WORD

Prayer for Illumination
Scripture
Sermon
Hymn, Psalm, or Spiritual Song
Affirmation of Faith
Invitation to Discipleship
Thanksgiving for Baptism
Prayers of Intercession

EUCHARIST

Invitation to Offering
Offering
Invitation to the Table
Great Thanksgiving
Communion
Prayer after Communion

[IF THE EUCHARIST IS OMITTED]

Invitation to Offering
Offering

Prayer of Thanksgiving

SENDING

Hymn, Psalm, or Spiritual Song
Blessing and *Charge*

This order of worship is offered as one example. The actions and elements of worship may of course be arranged in a variety of other ways according to denominational patterns and congregational practices. This resource is also available in ebook format, from which users can copy and paste liturgies for use in bulletins and other worship materials.

Lectionary Readings

This resource is designed to support and equip users of the three-year Revised Common Lectionary (1992), developed by the ecumenical Consultation on Common Texts as an adaptation and expansion of the Common Lectionary (1983). The contents and composition of this volume reflect that emphasis, consistent with the Connections commentary series.

However, this resource also includes supplemental liturgical materials for the four-year Narrative Lectionary (2010), designed by faculty at Luther Seminary in St. Paul, Minnesota. Taking advantage of overlap between the two systems, with these supplemental materials, this resource will address (at least obliquely) all of the primary texts of the Narrative Lectionary over the course of its six volumes.

See the Scripture index for the list of the lectionary readings supported in this volume (in canonical order). A comprehensive biblical index for both lectionaries will be published when all six volumes of the *Connections Worship Companion* have been completed.

Acknowledgments

Contributors to this volume include Claudia L. Aguilar Rubalcava, Mamie Broadhurst, Marci Auld Glass, Marcus A. Hong, Kimberly Bracken Long, Emily McGinley, Kendra L. Buckwalter Smith, Samuel Son, Slats Toole, and Byron A. Wade. Their deep faith, pastoral wisdom, creative gifts, and fervent prayers are the lifeblood of this work. The editor also expresses deep gratitude to David Maxwell, vice president for curriculum and church resources at Westminster John Knox Press, for his guidance in the development of this project, and to Jessica Miller Kelley, senior acquisitions editor at Westminster John Knox Press, for shepherding it to completion.

Key to Symbols and Abbreviations

Regular	Leader
Bold	People
Italics	Rubric describing liturgical action or identifying options
. . .	Time for individual prayers, spoken or silent
or	Alternate readings or responses

Resources for the Revised Common Lectionary

SEASON OF ADVENT

Making Connections

The season of Advent is a time for preparation. With hope and longing, we prepare to welcome the coming realm of God and the glorious return of our Savior. With wonder and joy, we prepare to celebrate the nativity of Jesus and the mystery of the incarnation. During these Advent days, we make way for Christ's coming.

The Gospel of Mark begins with the theme of preparation. Mark recalls the prophecy of Isaiah, "See, I am sending my messenger ahead of you, who will prepare your way; the voice of one crying out in the wilderness: 'Prepare the way of the Lord'" (Mark 1:2–3; cf. Isa. 40:3). Unlike the other evangelists, Mark provides no birth narrative, no grand genealogy, no poetic prologue. This Gospel plunges us into the story "immediately" (one of Mark's favorite words). John the baptizer is already waiting in the wilderness. The life and mission of Jesus are already underway. Ironically, perhaps, the reader has little time to prepare.

The Revised Common Lectionary Year B focuses on the Gospel of Mark, the shortest of the four canonical Gospels and the first to be written, according to scholarly consensus. Because Mark is shorter and lacks some of the accounts of Jesus' life and ministry provided by the other evangelists, Year B sometimes supplements Mark with passages from the other Gospels, particularly around Christmas, Easter, and in the time after Pentecost. Yet Mark has its own structure and style, propelled by an action-packed narrative, the fulfillment of time, and the in-breaking of the reign of God.

As you keep watch and prepare for worship this Advent season, remember the immediacy and urgency of Mark. People are hungry, hurting, homeless. Friends and family are sick and suffering. Nations and neighborhoods are plagued by violence. Earth is groaning for renewal. Now is the time for fervent prayer and bold action. Now is the time to "repent, and believe in the good news" (Mark 1:15).

Christ is coming! Prepare the way of the Lord.

Seasonal/Repeating Resources

These resources are intended for regular use throughout the season of Advent.

CONFESSION AND PARDON

The confession and pardon may be led from the baptismal font.

> When we turn to the Lord in our hearts,
> God speaks peace to us.
>
> Trusting in God's faithfulness and steadfast love,
> let us confess our sin.

The confession may begin with a time of silence for personal prayer.

> **God of the past, present, and future,**
> **we praise you for your presence in our lives.**
> **We confess that we have turned away from you.**
> **Our hearts are devoted to the desires of the flesh.**
> **Our thoughts focus on our own needs**
> **at the expense of others.**
> **Our minds are occupied with what is happening**
> **in our lives at this moment**
> **instead of focusing on your calling.**
>
> **In your mercy, forgive us, O God.**
> **Through the power of your Holy Spirit,**
> **turn us away from our own desires**
> **and turn us toward your will;**
> **through Jesus Christ we pray.**

Water may be poured or lifted from the baptismal font.

Steadfast love and faithfulness will meet;
righteousness and peace will kiss each other.
Faithfulness will spring up from the ground,
and righteousness will look down from the sky.

In the name of Jesus Christ, we are forgiven.
Thanks be to God.

PRAYER FOR ILLUMINATION

The prayer for illumination is led from the lectern or pulpit.

Eternal God, by your Holy Spirit
and through these prophetic writings,
reveal to us the mystery of the ages,
teach us to be faithful to your will,
and strengthen us according to the gospel
of Jesus Christ our Savior. **Amen.**

THANKSGIVING FOR BAPTISM

The thanksgiving for baptism is led from the baptismal font.

*The introductory dialogue ("The Lord be with you . . .") may be sung
or spoken.*

Glory to you, O God,
Alpha and Omega.

In the beginning of creation,
you sent your Spirit over the water
and called all things into being
through the voice of your Word.

In the beginning of Jesus' ministry,
you poured out your Holy Spirit upon him
and claimed him as your Beloved,
your Word made flesh to dwell among us.

At the beginning of this new year
in the life and mission of your church,
fill us with the power of your Spirit,
that we may bear witness to your Word.

Keep us faithful to the end,
living according to the promise of our baptism
until Christ comes in glory
to establish your realm of justice and peace.

Glory to you, O God,
Alpha and Omega. **Amen.**

GREAT THANKSGIVING

The Great Thanksgiving is led from the Communion table.

*The introductory dialogue ("The Lord be with you . . .") may be sung
or spoken.*

O Lord our God, how great is your love
and how wonderful is your name!
You created this world
and provide all we need to live.
You call us to be your people
and lead us as a flock.
You turn tears into laughter
and fill us with good things.
When we lose our way
you send prophets to call us home.

In hope we sing your praise:

The Sanctus ("Holy, holy, holy . . .") may be sung or spoken.

We give thanks that you sent Jesus
to be born and live among us
as a gift of your love and grace.
We confess that we rejected him
and allowed him to be crucified.
Yet we rejoice that his death was not the end
and that his resurrection brings a new creation.

The words of institution are included here, if not elsewhere, while the bread and cup are lifted (but not broken/poured).

> With great thanksgiving, O Lord,
> we remember your love for all people
> revealed in Jesus Christ.
> As we break this bread and drink this cup,
> we offer ourselves in service to you
> from this day to the end of the age.

A memorial acclamation ("Christ has died . . .") may be sung or spoken.

> Pour out your Holy Spirit, O Lord,
> upon these gifts of bread and wine,
> and upon us as your people,
> that together we may be the body and blood
> of our Lord Jesus Christ.
>
> Empower us by your Holy Spirit
> to live as one people in the world.
> Help us to live in peace and joy
> until Christ comes again.

A Trinitarian doxology and Great Amen may be sung or spoken.

PRAYER AFTER COMMUNION

The prayer after Communion is led from the Communion table.

> Gracious God, we give you thanks
> for this meal we have shared.
> Strengthen us through this bread and cup
> to serve you with love, peace, and compassion.
> Lead us to live in joyful expectation
> until the coming of Jesus Christ,
> your Son and our Savior. **Amen.**

PRAYER OF THANKSGIVING

The prayer of thanksgiving may be led from the Communion table.

Almighty God, in Jesus Christ
we have witnessed your saving work.
We give you thanks and praise
that you have guided us in the past,
you still guide us in the present,
and you will guide us into the future.
We thank you for all the blessings
you have provided in this life,
especially for the gift of your love
and the calling to share that love with others.
Especially we thank you for Jesus Christ,
who came to dwell among us
and has shown us your way of life.
With hope and prayer, we await his return
on the day when your righteousness
will reign over the whole world.
Until that glorious day,
fill us with your love and mercy.
Help us to be a thankful people,
rejoicing in your service;
through Jesus Christ our Lord. **Amen.**

BLESSING

The blessing and charge may be led from the doors of the church.

May God Most High look upon you with favor,
may the Holy Spirit overshadow you,
and may it be with you according to God's Word. **Alleluia!**

First Sunday of Advent

Isaiah 64:1–9
Psalm 80:1–7, 17–19

1 Corinthians 1:3–9
Mark 13:24–37

OPENING SENTENCES

> When God performs deeds
> that we did not expect,
> it is God coming down to be among us.
> **Mountains quake and hearts are changed.**
>
> Let the God of the unexpected
> be among us today.
> **Let us worship God.**

PRAYER OF THE DAY

> Faithful God, tear open the heavens
> and come to dwell among us,
> that we might be enlivened by your presence.
> Reveal your ever-present activity among us,
> that our hearts may be renewed
> and our minds inspired to join your mission.
> Work with us, as the potter works with clay,
> that we might be molded for your good purposes.
> We pray in the name of Christ,
> who draws close to us,
> that we might draw closer to you, our God. **Amen.**

Yet, O LORD, you are our Father; we are the clay, and you are our potter; we are all the work of your hand.

Isaiah 64:8

INVITATION TO DISCIPLESHIP

The invitation to discipleship may be led from the baptismal font.

> We are yet-unfinished clay,
> ready to be molded for a worthy purpose
> in God's new creation.
>
> If you would like to be crafted by the Master Artist
> who sees all of what we can be,
> give yourself over for transformation
> and see what God will do with you!

PRAYERS OF INTERCESSION

The prayers of intercession may be led from the midst of the congregation.

> Compassionate God,
> you see our pain and still choose to come close.
> Stir up within us a deep awareness
> of how we might live and serve with your compassion,
> even in a world that entices us toward despair.
> Come close, dwell among us, and receive our prayer.
>
> We pray for our neighborhoods . . .
> that our alienation might be healed
> and torn social fabrics might be mended.
> Help us to reach out, make connections,
> and extend your gracious hospitality,
> remembering that you work alongside us.
>
> For our towns and cities . . .
> that we might pay attention to the referendums,
> policy changes, budgetary decisions, and rhetoric
> that shape our collective social imaginations.
> Help us to be voices of your grace
> and agents of your restorative justice.
>
> For our nation and world . . .
> that we might see what you see
> in one another and in the broader world
> that you are seeking to cultivate.
> Let us not become cynical or withdrawn,
> but follow your lead and incline our ears
> to those who suffer under oppression and injustice.

God who not only sees and listens but also acts:
We long for your restorative work within and around us.
Help us to remember that
as we wait with Advent hope,
this an active waiting.
Grant us your power—
rooted in deep love,
fueled by gospel courage,
and sustained with prophetic joy,
living in the world that is
even as we watch and work for the world to come;
in Jesus' name. **Amen.**

INVITATION TO OFFERING

The invitation to offering may be led from the Communion table.

All that we have belongs to God.
Despite what we have been told and taught
about earthly economic structures,
we know that this is God's world.

Let us act on this truth together,
trusting that when we share our gifts,
God will do more through us
than we could ever do on our own.

INVITATION TO THE TABLE

The invitation to the table is led from the Communion table.

At this table, we remember that
while the world is not yet what it could be,
we have access to the history and hope
of all the faithful who came before us.
We are not alone on this path
of seeking a world where God's will is done.

In this season of Advent,
you are invited to activate your hope
by remembering God's story among us
and communing with those
who have gathered at this table
since the earliest days of the church.

CHARGE

The blessing and charge may be led from the doors of the church.

Go forth from this place with hope activated,
imagination stirred, and love renewed,
all for the renewing of the world.
Amen. *or* **Thanks be to God.**

Second Sunday of Advent

Isaiah 40:1–11   2 Peter 3:8–15a
Psalm 85:1–2, 8–13   Mark 1:1–8

OPENING SENTENCES

A voice cries out in the wilderness:
Prepare the way of the Lord.

Let us make straight in the desert
a highway for our God.
Let us worship God.

PRAYER OF THE DAY

God of comfort and might,
as we gather together,
mend us for your good purposes,
that we might have the courage
to speak your truths out loud
and the holy confidence
to live and love without fear;
in Christ's name we pray. **Amen.**

*But do not ignore this one fact, beloved, that with the
Lord one day is like a thousand years, and a thousand
years are like one day.*

2 Peter 3:8

INVITATION TO DISCIPLESHIP

The invitation to discipleship may be led from the baptismal font.

Friends, God is not slow in keeping promises
but is patient with us,
not wanting any to perish
but desiring that all people
may come to restored relationship—
with self, with one another, and with God.

Are you longing for relationships restored?
Come to Jesus and let him lead you
in the work of your healing
for the sake of a world made new.

PRAYERS OF INTERCESSION

The prayers of intercession may be led from the midst of the congregation.

God of comfort and mercy,
of restoration and forgiveness,
we ask that you accomplish within us
what you alone can do:
Forgive us and liberate us
from the ways that we have fallen short,
that we might know your forgiveness,
be restored to one another,
and be sent for your purposes in the world.
As we discern our next steps,
hear our prayers.

For those struggling with despair, depression, addiction,
and other mental health challenges during this season . . .

For those who are grappling with what it means
to believe that your promises are true,
when so many promises are left unfulfilled . . .

For those moving through this season for the first time
after experiencing loss and grief in their many forms . . .

For those among us who struggle and suffer
with pains that others do not know . . .

We give you thanks, O God,
that you see who we are where we are.
We entrust our longing to you.
Equip us to be people of compassion and grace,
that as we anticipate your coming,
we might already know the joy
of your presence and peace among us;
through Christ our Savior. **Amen.**

INVITATION TO OFFERING

The invitation to offering may be led from the Communion table.

Remember the words of the psalmist—
faithfulness comes up from the earth
and righteousness comes down from the sky.
In the faithful offering of ourselves
we participate in God's righteous work,
meeting in the middle.

Let us offer our lives and gifts to God,
for God has invited us to share
in the building of a new creation.

INVITATION TO THE TABLE

The invitation to the table is led from the Communion table.

At this table we remember and look forward,
joining the hopes of a long line of ancestors—
pilgrims of peace and purveyors of possibility.

Let us gather with saints of all times and places
to be renewed, reconciled, and repurposed
for God's good work in the world.

CHARGE

The blessing and charge may be led from the doors of the church.

> May the God who meets us
> in every phase of life and living
> grant us peace and empower us
> to offer grace and comfort
> for the world in which we live.
> **Amen.** *or* **Thanks be to God.**

Third Sunday of Advent

Isaiah 61:1–4, 8–11
Psalm 126 *or*
   Luke 1:46b–55

1 Thessalonians 5:16–24
John 1:6–8, 19–28

OPENING SENTENCES

> Rejoice, people of God!
> **The Lord is restoring our lives.**
>
> Those who sow in tears
> will reap with shouts of praise.
> **Those who go out weeping
> will come home with songs of joy.**

PRAYER OF THE DAY

> Lord God, you sent your servant John
> to testify to the light of Jesus Christ.
> Help us to heed the words of the prophets
> as we prepare the way
> for the new thing you are doing.
> Prepare your way in us,
> that our hearts may be ready
> for the coming of the Messiah;
> in whose holy name we pray. **Amen.**

INVITATION TO DISCIPLESHIP

The invitation to discipleship may be led from the baptismal font.

> The one who calls us is faithful.
> God will transform our lives
> to make us ready for the coming
> of the Lord Jesus Christ.
>
> Come to the God of peace.
> Bring all that you are—
> body, mind, and spirit—
> and God will make you new.

PRAYERS OF INTERCESSION

The prayers of intercession may be led from the midst of the congregation.

Lord God, send us your Spirit
to renew this weary, waiting world.
Hear our prayers.

Bring good news to the oppressed . . .
Come quickly to bring justice;
set all people free.

Bind up the brokenhearted . . .
Heal those who are sick and suffering;
sustain them by your grace.

Proclaim liberty to the captives . . .
Release those who are wrongly imprisoned;
break the chains of poverty and addiction.

Comfort those who mourn . . .
Support loved ones who are grieving;
fill them with your deep peace.

Rebuild the ancient ruins . . .
Restore our broken communities;
let them be places of safety and plenty.

Announce the year of your favor . . .
Show us glimpses of your new creation;
come among us here and now.

All this we pray in the name of Jesus,
the one anointed by your Spirit,
who comes to establish your holy realm
of righteousness, justice, and peace. **Amen.**

INVITATION TO OFFERING

The invitation to offering may be led from the Communion table.

Mary sang, "My soul magnifies the Lord,
and my spirit rejoices in God my Savior."
In Mary's vision of Christ's coming,
God looks with favor on the lowly,
casts the rich and mighty from their thrones,
and fills the hungry with good things.

Let us offer our lives to the Lord,
rejoicing in the God and Savior
who magnifies our gifts with grace.

INVITATION TO THE TABLE

The invitation to the table is led from the Communion table.

This is the table of the Lord,
where sorrow is transformed into joy—
where those who are hungry find a great feast;
where those in exile are welcomed home;
where a broken body is given
for the healing of the world.

Come to this table.
Christ invites you.
Come and join this joyful feast.

CHARGE

The blessing and charge may be led from the doors of the church.

Rejoice always, pray without ceasing,
and give thanks in all circumstances,
for this is the will of God in Christ Jesus for you.
Amen. *or* **Thanks be to God.**

Fourth Sunday of Advent

2 Samuel 7:1–11, 16
Luke 1:46b–55 *or*
  Psalm 89:1–4, 19–26

Romans 16:25–27
Luke 1:26–38

OPENING SENTENCES

We sing of the steadfast love of the Lord.
We proclaim God's faithfulness to all.

The faithfulness and steadfast love of God
have come to dwell among us in Jesus Christ.
**The Lord is our God,
the Rock of our salvation.**

PRAYER OF THE DAY

Holy One,
nothing is impossible with you.
By the power of your Spirit,
you sent the child of Mary
to be the redeemer of the world.
Look upon us with favor,
be with us this day and always,
and let it be with us according to your Word,
Jesus Christ our Savior. **Amen.**

INVITATION TO DISCIPLESHIP

The invitation to discipleship may be led from the baptismal font.

There was once a great mystery,
kept secret for long ages—
the mystery of God's purpose
in the history of the world.
Now the secret is revealed
with the coming of Jesus Christ.

In this season of Advent,
we invite you to meet Christ,
even as he comes to meet us.
Come and learn your purpose
in the life of the world God loves.

PRAYERS OF INTERCESSION

The prayers of intercession may be led from the midst of the congregation.

God of all history, God of all mystery,
we come before you in prayer
seeking your purpose for the world.

We pray for those without housing . . .
Help them find refuge and safety.

We pray for leaders of nations . . .
Give them wisdom to seek your will.

We pray for the meek and lowly . . .
Claim them as beloved and blessed.

We pray for the high and mighty . . .
Humble them to serve others.

We pray for children and youth . . .
Empower them to answer your call.

We pray for older people . . .
Satisfy them with dreams fulfilled.

We pray for those who wait . . .
Let them not lose hope.

We pray for those who work . . .
Equip them in building up your realm.

Help us to be faithful in serving you, O God.
Strengthen us according to the gospel
to proclaim the good news of Jesus,
to whom we give glory forever! **Amen.**

INVITATION TO OFFERING

The invitation to offering may be led from the Communion table.

King David wanted to build a house for God,
a great and glorious temple for the Lord.
But the Lord said: Do you not remember?
I am the one who called you from the pasture
and made you the shepherd of my people.
I am the one who will build a house
for you and your descendants forever.

God is the giver of life and every good thing.
God will build us up as the body of Christ
to be shelter and sanctuary for all people.
Let us offer our lives to the Lord.

INVITATION TO THE TABLE

The invitation to the table is led from the Communion table.

This is the table of Christ our Lord.
Here there is food for the hungry.
Here there is plenty for the poor.
Here there is welcome for the outcast.
Here there is justice for the oppressed.
Here there is favor for the forgotten.

Come to this table of grace.
Come, eat and drink in the presence
of the one who is coming in glory.

CHARGE

The blessing and charge may be led from the doors of the church.

Go forth to magnify the Lord,
rejoicing in God our Savior.
Nothing is impossible with God.
Amen. *or* **Thanks be to God.**

SEASON OF CHRISTMAS

Making Connections

The Christmas season begins with a "Silent Night" on the eve of the Nativity of the Lord (December 25), when we gather in hushed wonder at the cradle of God's Word made flesh. It concludes with "Joy to the World" on Epiphany (January 6), when we proclaim the good news that Christ is Savior and Lord of all the earth. During the twelve days in between, the church celebrates the incarnation and nativity of Jesus, the Messiah, with songs of thanks and praise.

Since the Gospel of Mark is silent about the birth of Jesus, Year B of the Revised Common Lectionary presents an excellent opportunity for reflection on the "Hymn to the Logos" at the opening of the Gospel of John. This poetic prologue to the life and ministry of Jesus appears as one of the lectionary readings for the Nativity of the Lord, as well as the second Sunday of Christmas on years when the twelve days include two Sundays.

Echoing the opening words of Genesis, "In the beginning," John sings the praise of the Wisdom or Word (Greek, *Logos*) of God who was present at the dawn of creation, bringing life and light to the world (John 1:1; cf. Gen. 1:1). The Gospel tells of one named John who was sent to bear witness to this light, that people might believe and become children of God. John testifies that God's Word has become flesh, living among us, full of grace and truth. Speech alone cannot contain such meaning and mystery; such wonders must be sung.

As you sing your way through this season, pay close attention to how the hymns of our faith testify to Jesus Christ. What images of Jesus do they reveal or conceal? How do they describe the wonder of Christ's incarnation, nativity, and epiphany? Which of the four Gospel writers do they favor? Which nativity stories do they recount? How do they bring light and life into our celebration of Christmas and help us believe the good news? Draw on these beloved songs in preaching, teaching, study, and prayer; they are a rich repository of memory, meaning, and mystery for the worshipers in your congregation.

With "Silent Night," "Joy to the World," and countless other classic carols, celebrate Christmas with singing, joining the song of the heavenly host.

Seasonal/Repeating Resources

These resources are intended for regular use throughout the season of Christmas.

CONFESSION AND PARDON

The confession and pardon may be led from the baptismal font.

> When the goodness and loving-kindness
> of God our Savior appeared, Jesus delivered us,
> not because of any works of righteousness we had done,
> but according to his great mercy,
> through the water of rebirth
> and renewal by the Holy Spirit.
>
> Trusting in God's grace, let us confess our sin.

The confession may begin with a time of silence for personal prayer.

> **Merciful God,**
> **we confess our sinfulness before you.**
> **We have tried to do what is right,**
> **but instead we have lived as people**
> **separated from your presence.**
> **We confess that we have not**
> **taken care of those in need.**
> **We confess that we are complicit**
> **in systems of oppression.**
> **We confess that we have hurt others**
> **and harmed ourselves.**

Loving God, in your mercy, forgive us.
Through the power of your Holy Spirit,
let us be reconciled to you
and live in a way that is worthy of your kingdom;
through Jesus Christ our Lord.

Water may be poured or lifted from the baptismal font.

Hear the good news.
God pours out the Spirit richly upon us
through Jesus Christ our Savior,
so that, having been justified by grace,
we might inherit the hope of eternal life.

In the name of Jesus Christ, we are forgiven.
Thanks be to God.

PRAYER FOR ILLUMINATION

The prayer for illumination is led from the lectern or pulpit.

Holy God,
shine your light on us this day
as your Word is read and proclaimed.
Send your Holy Spirit
to chase away the shadows
and make clear the path
you would have us take.
With shepherds and magi,
we are seeking you.
In Jesus' name we pray. **Amen.**

THANKSGIVING FOR BAPTISM

The thanksgiving for baptism is led from the baptismal font.

The introductory dialogue ("The Lord be with you . . .") may be sung or spoken.

In you, O God, we rejoice and give thanks,
for you have washed us in the waters of baptism,
covered us with the robe of your righteousness,
and clothed us with the garments of salvation.

Through these waters and by your Spirit
you have chosen and claimed us,
calling us by a new name: beloved child.

As the rain falls to water the earth,
bringing up new life from a garden,
cause righteousness, justice, and praise
to spring up among the nations.

Send us forth from these waters in peace,
according to your word,
proclaiming the good news of salvation
to all the peoples of the earth;
through Jesus Christ our Lord. **Amen.**

GREAT THANKSGIVING

The Great Thanksgiving is led from the Communion table.

The introductory dialogue ("The Lord be with you . . .") may be sung or spoken.

Blessed is your name, O Lord, in all the earth!
We give thanks and praise for all you have done—
for the gift of creation,
the wonder of all life,
the blessing of being in community,
and the promise of your everlasting presence.
Even when we have not been faithful,
you have kept covenant with us.
In the fullness of time, you sent your prophets
to prepare the way for the Messiah.

Therefore, we celebrate you with singing,
joining the hymn of the heavenly host:

The Sanctus ("Holy, holy, holy . . .") may be sung or spoken.

We give you thanks and praise for Jesus,
your Word made flesh, full of grace and truth.
He shared a life like ours,
felt human pain,
had compassion for the sick and needy,
spent time with sinners,
and confronted injustice,
proclaiming the coming of your realm.
Jesus was put to death on the cross
but rose to become our living Lord,
that we might be born anew
as your beloved children.

The words of institution are included here, if not elsewhere, while the bread and cup are lifted (but not broken/poured).

Remembering all your mighty works,
we share this bread and cup,
praying, "Come, Lord Jesus!"

A memorial acclamation ("Christ has died . . .") may be sung or spoken.

Come, Holy Spirit,
and be made known in the bread and cup,
and among those who are gathered at this table.

Make us one body in the church,
serving one mission in the world.
Send us forth to bear witness
to the good news of Jesus Christ,
especially among your people
who are hungry, poor, and oppressed.
May our lives be an example
of your love, grace, and mercy,
until Christ comes again to reign.

A Trinitarian doxology and Great Amen may be sung or spoken.

PRAYER AFTER COMMUNION

The prayer after Communion is led from the Communion table.

> God of all grace and goodness,
> we thank you for the gift of this meal
> we have shared together in Jesus' name.
> Help us to live as his faithful followers—
> sharing bread and good news with others,
> working for justice and peace in the world,
> and bearing witness to your love for all;
> through Christ, your Son and our Savior. **Amen.**

PRAYER OF THANKSGIVING

The prayer of thanksgiving may be led from the Communion table.

> God of wonder, you are the source
> of all things good and holy.
> We praise you for your creation,
> for friends, family, and other loved ones,
> for resources, time, and gifts to share,
> and neighbors with whom to share them.
> Above all, we praise you
> for the gift of Jesus Christ our Savior,
> whom we celebrate in this season.
> Keep us in your grace and peace,
> and teach us to live according to your way,
> that we may love and serve you all our days;
> through the power of your Holy Spirit
> and for the sake of Jesus Christ our Lord. **Amen.**

BLESSING

The blessing and charge may be led from the doors of the church.

> The blessing of Abba, the Father,
> the blessing of Jesus, the Son,
> and the blessing of the Holy Spirit
> be with you all, now and always. **Alleluia!**

Christmas Eve/Nativity of the Lord, Proper I

December 24

Isaiah 9:2–7   Titus 2:11–14
Psalm 96   Luke 2:1–14 (15–20)

OPENING SENTENCES

> O sing to the Lord a new song;
> sing to the Lord, all the earth.
> **Sing to the Lord, bless God's name;**
> **tell of God's salvation from day to day.**
>
> Declare God's glory among the nations,
> God's marvelous works among all the peoples.
> **For great is the Lord, and greatly to be praised!**

PRAYER OF THE DAY

> Emmanuel, God with us,
> like the shepherds we have come here looking for you,
> ready to glorify and praise you
> for all we have heard and seen.
> Your presence with your people, both long ago and today,
> brings to birth in us the hope, peace, joy, and love
> we wish for the whole world.
> May your angels quell any fears we might have,
> so we too can join this celebration
> with excitement and praise. **Amen.**

> *The people who walked in darkness have seen a great light; those who lived in a land of deep darkness—on them light has shined.*
>
> *Isaiah 9:2*

INVITATION TO DISCIPLESHIP

The invitation to discipleship may be led from the baptismal font.

Jesus Christ was born today!
It is news too wonderful to keep to ourselves.

How will you share the wonder
of a God who became one of us?
In what ways can you show God's love and justice
through your actions this week?
In what ways can you show the grace of God
through your zeal for good deeds this week?

PRAYERS OF INTERCESSION

The prayers of intercession may be led from the midst of the congregation.

O Holy One,
on this day when we celebrate your birth
we call out to you with prayers for those we know,
as well as those we do not know,
using a few of your many names.

Wonderful Counselor,
we pray this day for all who are in need of support.
We pray for all who feel sad or alone,
particularly at this time of year.
Messages of joy and love and hope and peace
may feel like promises to cling to,
or they may feel like gags
that keep harder feelings from being voiced.
May we allow space for every heart here,
whether it be filled to bursting
or struggling to beat.

Mighty God,
we pray for those who are afraid:
for those who live in homes
that are not safe, or warm, or assured;
for those who worry their addiction may win;
for those whose jobs are on the line;
for those whose lives are in danger
because they make others uncomfortable.

In Scripture, the angel comes to those in fear
and says, "Do not be afraid!"
May we come alongside any who need those same words
and find ways to make the angel's message come alive.

Everlasting One,
we pray for those who have lost loved ones this year,
or those who are watching their loved ones slip away.
It is hard, particularly at this time of year,
to have an empty seat at the table
or to miss the sound of someone's laughter.
May the knowledge of your eternal care
for us and for all we love
offer comfort and even joy in this season.

Prince of Peace,
it is not in the workings of this world
that we place our trust; our trust is in you.
As wars rage and divisions deepen,
may your Spirit help us find ways to draw together.
We pray today for peace throughout the world,
especially in [*particular places may be named*].
May all people know peace
and all lands find rest from fighting.
May any peace that comes
not be simply the absence of fighting,
but a peace that rests on a foundation of justice
so that it might be a lasting peace.

God, let your light and love shine upon us
this day and forevermore. **Amen.**

INVITATION TO OFFERING

The invitation to offering may be led from the Communion table.

God's greatest offering comes to us this day.
Let the heavens be glad, and let the earth rejoice;
let the sea roar and all that fills it.
Let us also show our gratitude.

Let us return our gifts of time, talent, and treasure
to God and God's people.

INVITATION TO THE TABLE

The invitation to the table is led from the Communion table.

Friends, the wait is over.

We meet at this table
to wonder at the miracle of God's presence with us.
We meet one another here,
and we meet Christ here,
for it is his table.
Let us prepare to welcome Jesus once again,
for he is the one who always welcomes us.

CHARGE

The blessing and charge may be led from the doors of the church.

Go into the world looking for Christ's presence among us.
Jesus Christ is born today!
Do not be afraid.
Glory to God in the highest heaven, and on earth peace.
Amen. *or* **Thanks be to God.**

Christmas Day/Nativity of the Lord, Proper II

December 25

Isaiah 62:6–12   Titus 3:4–7
Psalm 97   Luke 2:(1–7) 8–20

OPENING SENTENCES

> You, O Lord, are most high over all the earth;
> you are exalted far above all gods.
> **The Lord loves those who hate evil;**
> **God guards the lives of the faithful**
> **and rescues them from the hand of the wicked.**
>
> Light dawns for the righteous,
> and joy for the upright in heart.
> **Rejoice in the Lord, O you righteous,**
> **and give thanks to God's holy name!**

PRAYER OF THE DAY

> God of all things living,
> your coming is a joy for all creation,
> from the coastlands to the mountains,
> the heavens and the earth.
> As we gather together this day,
> help us to feel the joy that pulses through all things
> and to catch a glimpse of all that could be.
> In Jesus' name we pray. **Amen.**

> *And suddenly there was with the angel a multitude of the heavenly host, praising God and saying, "Glory to God in the highest heaven, and on earth peace among those whom [God] favors!"*
>
> *Luke 2:13–14*

INVITATION TO DISCIPLESHIP

The invitation to discipleship may be led from the baptismal font.

The psalmist tells us
that the Lord loves those who hate evil;
God guards the lives of the faithful
and rescues them from the hands of the wicked.

Jesus showed us how to embody the work of God.
Now we are the hands and feet of God.
How will we help guard the lives of others,
and how might we accept the care of others for us?

PRAYERS OF INTERCESSION

The prayers of intercession may be led from the midst of the congregation.

Worship leaders may wish to change the order or wording of this prayer according to the themes or images highlighted in the weeks of Advent.

Eternal God,
you who have always existed,
and whose birth we celebrate today,
we bring before you our hopes and fears,
our joys and concerns,
our desires and our divisions.
We bring them to the foot of the manger
as an offering of faith:
for on this day hope was born.

The family you chose, God,
did not fit the rules of their day,
but they fit your rule.
They entrusted themselves to you,
and they cared for one another.
We pray for all who are told their families do not count,
for all who are asked to hide parts of themselves
in order to be accepted,
for all who feel they are not enough
or that they are not worthy.
We bring them to the foot of the manger
as an offering of faith:
for on this day love was born.

It was not to rulers that your birth was first announced,
but to shepherds—
people who were overlooked
and far from the halls of power.
May the gift of your presence—
the good news of great joy—
be heralded once again to all who are overlooked today:
for those who are unhoused,
for the uninsured or underinsured,
for those struggling with severe mental illness,
for people working multiple jobs to try to make ends meet.
We bring them to the foot of the manger
as an offering of faith:
for on this day joy was born.

You were born into a world of empire,
where those in charge could require vulnerable people
to make dangerous journeys.
Even today, sacrifices are asked of those
who cannot afford to give more.
May the story of your birth teach us
that things are supposed to be different:
that nations can lay down their weapons of war,
that there is enough food for everyone
to have something to eat,
that many diseases are preventable
with clean water and sanitation,
that the voices and stories of all people
are precious and to be valued.
We bring these possibilities to the foot of the manger
as an offering of faith:
for on this day peace was born.

Your birth brings us hope, love, joy, and peace.
May the lives we lead
continue to announce those promises to others.
In Jesus' name we pray. **Amen.**

INVITATION TO OFFERING

The invitation to offering may be led from the Communion table.

On this day the goodness and loving-kindness
of God our Savior appeared in human form.
Jesus Christ,
the baby who would grow and show us how to live,
gave his own life for us.
He saved us,
not because of any works of righteousness that we had done,
but according to his mercy.

May that mercy inspire our own giving
of our time, our talents, and our treasure—
all for the glory of God.

INVITATION TO THE TABLE

The invitation to the table is led from the Communion table.

This table is for you.
This table is for me.
This table is for him.
This table is for her.
This table is for them.
This table is for us.

This table is God's table,
and because we are all God's people,
we are all invited.
Welcome to this table of grace, friends.
Come, and enjoy the feast.

CHARGE

The blessing and charge may be led from the doors of the church.

Friends, every place is God's place.
There is no place you can go
where God is unwilling or unable to go as well.
Look for God everywhere you go,
and God will find you.
Let us go out, rejoicing and giving thanks to God!
Amen. *or* **Thanks be to God.**

Christmas Day/Nativity of the Lord, Proper III

December 25

Isaiah 52:7–10   Hebrews 1:1–4 (5–12)
Psalm 98   John 1:1–14

OPENING SENTENCES

How beautiful upon the mountains
are the feet of the messenger who announces peace,
who brings good news, who announces salvation,
who says to Zion, "Your God reigns."
The Lord has brought comfort to all people.
Let us break forth into singing,
for God has done marvelous things!

PRAYER OF THE DAY

God of the manger,
we join the floods as they clap their hands.
We join the hills as they sing for joy.
Together we rejoice,
for you have come to earth this day.
Heaven and earth have met in you.
Light and life,
Word made flesh,
beginning and end,
we welcome you this day,
singing your praises now and forevermore.
In Jesus' name we pray. **Amen.**

> *Make a joyful noise to the LORD, all the earth;*
> *break forth into joyous song and sing praises.*
>
> *Psalm 98:4*

INVITATION TO DISCIPLESHIP

The invitation to discipleship may be led from the baptismal font.

We can treasure the darkness,
even as we welcome the light.
It is in the darkness that life begins—
deep in the soil,
safe in the womb.

Take a walk in the light this week,
and then walk that same path again in the dark.
Notice how those walks are different.
What do you notice on each occasion?
How well are you aware of what is around you
during the day and during the night?
Do you notice God's presence with you more
at one time or another?

PRAYERS OF INTERCESSION

The prayers of intercession may be led from the midst of the congregation.

Gracious God,
as we come together to celebrate your birth in Jesus,
we also come together
to bring our joys and concerns to you.

God, we thank you
for the many gifts you have offered us.
We thank you for the gift of your Son Jesus—
for joining us in the flesh and living among us,
sharing every bit of our experience.
You lived the joy of friendship and family;
you knew the power of love and healing;
you saw the wonder of meals shared and lives transformed.
So we come to you now with gratitude
for the many ways we have experienced your blessings—
some of which are known to everyone here,
and some of which are known only to us.

Listen, O God, as we lift our prayers silently to you . . .

God, mixed in with our many blessings
have been moments of deep pain and sorrow.
We know you understand that as well.
We know that, in Christ, you have been betrayed.
You have had friends die.
You have seen injustice at work.
Though in Jesus you lived your life
to make earth as it is in heaven,
you were not accepted
and perhaps never really known.
Your life is a testament to the ups and downs
we all know so well.
So we come to share the worries
of our minds and our hearts with you—
some of which are known to everyone here,
and some of which are known only to us.

Listen, O God, as we lift our prayers silently to you . . .

God, may the promise of your presence with us,
so many years ago and even today,
offer us the light and life we need
to continue your work in the world today.
May your example of grace and truth in Jesus
be the gift we give now and evermore. **Amen.**

INVITATION TO OFFERING

The invitation to offering may be led from the Communion table.

The Word has been with us since the beginning.
A gift from eternity to eternity.
Today we celebrate that Word in human form—
as a babe lying in a manger.
The gift we have been given
is one that also asks us to care for others.

May we use the time, the talents,
and the treasure entrusted to us
as a way of offering our thanks for the gift of Christ.

INVITATION TO THE TABLE

The invitation to the table is led from the Communion table.

> God comes to us in many ways:
> as an infant, holy yet vulnerable;
> in the movement of the Spirit, wild and free;
> at this table, through the gifts of bread and cup.
> Jesus was born in Bethlehem many years ago.
> The Spirit leads us into the future.
>
> And God joins us here, at this table, now.
> Come, let us join the feast God has prepared.
> All are invited.

CHARGE

The blessing and charge may be led from the doors of the church.

> As you go forth,
> remember that Christmas is not just one day but a season.
> May the next twelve days be filled with God's light,
> with the joy of God's presence,
> and with moments that bring your heart to song.
> Merry Christmas!
> **Amen.** *or* **Thanks be to God.**

First Sunday after Christmas Day

December 26—January 1

Isaiah 61:10–62:3   Galatians 4:4–7
Psalm 148   Luke 2:22–40

OPENING SENTENCES

Praise the Lord!
Praise the Lord from the heavens;
praise God in the heights!
Praise God, all the angels!

Praise God, sun and moon and shining stars!
**Praise the Lord from the earth,
you sea monsters and all deeps!**

Mountains and all hills,
fruit trees and all cedars!
**Wild animals and all cattle,
creeping things and flying birds!**

Kings of the earth and all peoples,
princes and all rulers of the earth!
**Young men and women alike,
old and young together!**

God's glory is above earth and heaven!
Let us praise the name of the Lord!

PRAYER OF THE DAY

Loving God,
as we celebrate your birth this Christmastide,
may we continue looking for you in the world around us.
As you did with Simeon,
help our eyes to see your salvation,
and may that lead us to ever more praise.
In Jesus' name we pray. **Amen.**

INVITATION TO DISCIPLESHIP

The invitation to discipleship may be led from the baptismal font.

Mary and Joseph took Jesus to the temple in Jerusalem.
While they were there, the prophet Anna saw him
and began to praise God and speak about Jesus
to all who were looking for redemption in Jerusalem.

How might we follow in Anna's footsteps this week?
How might we bring the joy we find in the birth of Jesus
to others who are also looking for a reorientation?

PRAYERS OF INTERCESSION

The prayers of intercession may be led from the midst of the congregation.

Jesus, Emmanuel, God with us,
we look and listen and see your reflection
in the world all around us.
You are in the majesty of the mountains.
You are in the thick undergrowth of the forests
and the soothing breeze of the bayou.
You are in the newborn baby's cry
and in the soothing whisper of a loved one's care.
You are in the grandparent's mischievous wink
and the mystery of a teenage glance.
We have each seen you in different ways,
whether we realized it or not at the time,
so we stop for a moment now to reflect
and bring to mind those moments—
glimpses we have had of you this week,
when our spirits have been lifted
or beauty has overcome us.

A time of silence follows for reflection and personal prayer.

Jesus, Emmanuel, God with us,
though we know that we are never alone,
still sometimes we feel that way.
The doctor gives us bad news,
and it seems no one else can possibly understand.
The bills mount up,
and we don't know where to turn.

The depression returns,
and we feel we shouldn't burden anyone else
with the weight of our despair.
We wrap ourselves up in our grief or our pain
in the hope that will feel like your loving embrace,
but it is not the same.
We cannot look for you
because our eyes are too full of tears.
We cannot listen for you
because our cries echo too loudly.
We have all felt alone at one time or another,
so we stop for a moment now
to reflect and bring to mind those moments—
as an act of solidarity, if nothing else—
when our spirits have been overwhelmed
and we have not known which way to turn to you.

A time of silence follows for reflection and personal prayer.

Jesus, Emmanuel, God with us,
whether we recognize you or not, you are there.
Allow those of us who have seen and felt your presence
to reach out, extending your love and your grace
to others as freely as you have given them to us.
And allow those of us who have missed you—
we who feel only numb, or whose spirits have sunk low—
to see the outstretched hand or read the kind text message
for just what they are:
a reminder that we are not alone
and that we are precious to you and your people.

Jesus, Emmanuel, God with us,
from the story of your birth
we have learned that it takes a village
to know the fullness of your presence.
Even after the miracle of your birth,
it is when the old man cradles the child,
and when the prophet sees your face,
that your parents are amazed all over again—
that they see you anew.
May we too see you anew, again,
this day and always. **Amen.**

INVITATION TO OFFERING

The invitation to offering may be led from the Communion table.

Just as Jesus' parents came
to present him to God in the temple,
we have come today
to bring our very selves to God.
We have come, ready to celebrate, perhaps,
or looking for something,
but we have also come with gifts
we can share with God and God's people.

Let us each offer the gifts we have—
gifts of time, talent, and treasure—
to the one who gave everything for us.

INVITATION TO THE TABLE

The invitation to the table is led from the Communion table.

Today we have the opportunity
to come before God at this table.
We do not have to bring any money to this table.
We do not have to bring any accomplishments to this table.
We do not have to bring any special talents to this table.
We only have to bring ourselves.

So please, come.
Bring your whole self.
Join Jesus at his table.
All are welcome.

CHARGE

The blessing and charge may be led from the doors of the church.

The words of the psalmist were our call to worship.
Now they are a charge for how we are called to live.

Praise the Lord!
Praise the Lord from the heavens;
praise God in the heights!
Praise God, all the angels!

Praise God, sun and moon and shining stars!
Praise the Lord from the earth,
you sea monsters and all deeps!

Mountains and all hills,
fruit trees and all cedars!
Wild animals and all cattle,
creeping things and flying birds!

Kings of the earth and all peoples,
princes and all rulers of the earth!
Young men and women alike,
old and young together!

God's glory is above earth and heaven!
Let us praise the name of the Lord!
Amen. *or* **Thanks be to God.**

Second Sunday after Christmas Day

January 2–5

Jeremiah 31:7–14 *or*
   Sirach 24:1–12
Psalm 147:12–20 *or*
   Wisdom 10:15–21

Ephesians 1:3–14
John 1:(1–9) 10–18

OPENING SENTENCES

> Hear the word of the Lord, O nations,
> and declare it in the coastlands far away;
> **the one who scattered the people will gather them**
> **and will keep them as a shepherd tends a flock.**
>
> Their life shall become like a watered garden,
> and they shall never languish again.
> **The Lord will turn their mourning into joy**
> **and will comfort them,**
> **giving them gladness for sorrow.**
>
> Come, let us sing aloud to God
> **and be radiant over the goodness of the Lord.**

*In the beginning was the Word, and the Word was with God,
and the Word was God. He was in the beginning with God.
All things came into being through him, and without him
not one thing came into being. What has come into being in
him was life, and the life was the light of all people.*

John 1:1–4

PRAYER OF THE DAY

God of grace and truth,
out of the mysterious mists of eternity
you have shown us your glory,
covering your people in Wisdom
and clothing your Word in flesh.
As you gather us in your presence,
make your home in our hearts,
that guided along your marvelous way,
we might set our hope on Christ anew
and live for the praise of his glory. **Amen.**

INVITATION TO DISCIPLESHIP

The invitation to discipleship may be led from the baptismal font.

Christ came to his own,
and his own people did not accept him.
But to all who receive him
and who believe in his name,
he has given power to become children of God.

If you seek a love that spans eternity,
come to the one who calls you "beloved child."
If you seek the comfort and joy of home,
come to the one who made a home among us.
If you seek to be accepted just as you are,
come to the one who chose you
before the foundation of the world.

PRAYERS OF INTERCESSION

The prayers of intercession may be led from the midst of the congregation.

Abiding God,
you made this earth your home,
and its people your household.
As your beloved children we pray
to the praise of your glory.

Abide with your church, O Lord . . .
Enliven our response to your presence and call,
as a garden watered with refreshing rains,
lush with diversity,
bearing witness of your creative beauty
and rooted in your word.
As your beloved children we pray
to the praise of your glory.

Abide throughout the earth, O Lord . . .
Bring restoration to the habitations of all creatures.
Call us again to disciplined and attentive care
of the land we call home,
that all may be satisfied with your bounty
and know the riches of your grace.
As your beloved children we pray
to the praise of your glory.

Abide among the nations . . .
Open the hearts of people and leaders,
that every land may be a place of welcome and acceptance
for all who seek refuge and a place to call home.
Lead us in a straight path, and guide our stumbling feet
in seeking your kingdom here among us.
As your beloved children we pray
to the praise of your glory.

Abide with our loved ones . . .
Comfort those who are suffering,
turn their mourning into joy,
and let them trade all sorrow for gladness.
Redeem those captured by worry or struggle,
pain or addiction too strong for them,
and draw each of us close to your heart.
As your beloved children we pray
to the praise of your glory.

Abiding God, make your dwelling place among us
until that day when all things in heaven and on earth
are gathered up in Christ
and this world stands holy and blameless before you in love;
through Jesus Christ our Lord. **Amen.**

INVITATION TO OFFERING

The invitation to offering may be led from the Communion table.

God has blessed us in Christ
with every spiritual blessing in the heavenly places
and has lavished upon us the riches of grace.

As God's own children,
let us offer our lives and our gifts,
and with grateful hearts
extend such grace to others.

INVITATION TO THE TABLE

The invitation to the table is led from the Communion table.

This is the table of the Lord, who declares,
"See, I am going to bring them from the land of the north,
and gather them from the farthest parts of the earth."

Come, you who are scattered,
for at this table God gathers the beloved children.
Come, you who are weeping,
for at this table God trades gladness for sorrow.
Come, you who are wandering,
for at this table God welcomes us home.

Beloved of God, the grain and the wine are here.
We shall be radiant over the goodness of the Lord.

Children of God, a place is prepared for you here.
We shall receive from Christ's fullness grace upon grace.

CHARGE

The blessing and charge may be led from the doors of the church.

Christ has gathered us home in his presence,
that we may see the glory of the Lord,
full of grace and truth.
Know that as you go from this place,
you carry with you the Wisdom and the Word
of the one who has made a home in your heart.
Amen. *or* **Thanks be to God.**

Epiphany of the Lord

January 6 (or previous Sunday)

Isaiah 60:1–6   Ephesians 3:1–12
Psalm 72:1–7, 10–14   Matthew 2:1–12

OPENING SENTENCES

Arise, shine; for your light has come,
and the glory of the Lord has risen upon you.

For darkness shall cover the earth,
and thick darkness the peoples;

but the Lord will arise upon you,
and God's glory will appear over you.

Nations shall come to your light,
and kings to the brightness of your dawn.

PRAYER OF THE DAY

We are here, Holy One,
seeking your light, your glory, your revelation.
Center our spirits in you,
that we may rest in your mysteries,
confident that your light can chase away
the shadows that weigh us down,
and hopeful that what seems unclear now
is being worked out in your time.
We are here to pay you homage,
offer our gifts, and follow your star. **Amen.**

INVITATION TO DISCIPLESHIP

The invitation to discipleship may be led from the baptismal font.

If you're looking for a community
that seeks to follow God's star,
there is a place for you here.

Trust that the mystery of God
has brought you this far on your journey
and will guide your future steps.
All of who you are is welcome here.

PRAYERS OF INTERCESSION

The prayers of intercession may be led from the midst of the congregation.

Holy God,
like the wise ones, we seek you.
Some days you are easy to find;
the star shines bright and the path seems clear.
On other days we lose our way
when storms obscure the skies,
and we hunker down, seeking shelter,
uncertain when we will resume our journey.
No matter the weather, we are your children,
and we long to move closer to you.

So when the way is clear,
may our gratitude be loudly voiced and point us toward
extending grace toward others.
For the gift of this day,
and the joy of gathered community,
we give you thanks.

Particular thanksgivings may be named.

The leader may invite worshipers to share thanksgivings, saying:
"People of God, for what else do we offer our thanks this day?"

And when the storm clouds gather on the horizon,
when we lose sight of your star
and we feel alone and afraid,
send us reminders of your provision and care.
We offer prayers for those under the clouds
of illness and disease, grief and anxiety.
Break through the clouds,
and give our seeking hearts a glimpse of your glory.

Particular concerns may be named.

The leader may invite worshipers to share concerns, saying:
"People of God, for what else do we offer our prayers this day?"

The story of Herod demonstrates
that when bad leaders are afraid,
all of their subjects live in fear too.
We offer prayers for our world,
and for people who are called to lead.
May we be led by our hopes and not our fears.
May we build societies where people aren't subject
to the whims of insecure leaders
but are nurtured into wholeness and peace.

If we follow you,
the journey may take us home by other roads.
Increase our tolerance for change
and our willingness to be on unfamiliar roads.
Give us your courage in our seeking hearts.

We offer these prayers in the name of Christ Jesus our Lord,
in whom we have access to you in boldness and confidence
through our faith in him. **Amen.**

INVITATION TO OFFERING

The invitation to offering may be led from the Communion table.

The prophet Isaiah calls us to imagine a world
where families gather from the corners of the earth,
celebrating together in peace;
where people won't be hungry
because the abundance of the earth will be shared;
where nations will come toward God's light
and peace will be our companion.
When we give our offerings of time, talent, and treasure,
we join together in making that vision come true.

Confident in God's goodness,
let us share out of our abundance with grateful hearts.
We offer our gifts, our lives, and our hopes to God in joy.

INVITATION TO THE TABLE

The invitation to the table is led from the Communion table.

At this table we gather to be fed,
nourished, restored, and renewed.
By the mystery of God's grace,
these simple gifts of bread and cup
become a feast of abundant life
and this table has room enough for all.

Come and be fed for the journey.
There is room for you here.

CHARGE

The blessing and charge may be led from the doors of the church.

Go into the world, passionately followng the star.
Go into the world, sharing your light for others,
that they may see God through your joy.
Go into the world, knowing God has equipped you
with gifts that will bring light to the world.
Amen. *or* **Thanks be to God.**

TIME AFTER THE EPIPHANY

Making Connections

Between the seasons of Christmas and Lent the church observes six to nine weeks of "Ordinary Time," or the Time after the Epiphany. This span of time in the Christian year begins with the Baptism of the Lord, in which a voice from heaven proclaims that Jesus is God's beloved Son, and ends with the Transfiguration of the Lord, in which disciples witness the glory of God revealed in the presence of Christ. Throughout the intervening Sundays, the Gospel readings highlight scenes from the beginning of Jesus' ministry—the calling of his first followers, accounts of his teaching, and stories of his miraculous work.

In all three years of the Revised Common Lectionary, the Time after the Epiphany features readings from First and Second Corinthians. Year B is no exception. Paul's epistles to the church at Corinth demonstrate the blessings and burdens of life in Christian community—the same celebrations and challenges that would have been evident among Jesus' first disciples and that have continuing relevance in the lives of congregations and believers today.

Consider a few examples. On the second Sunday after the Epiphany, Paul weighs the difference between what may be lawful in the freedom of the Spirit and what is truly beneficial to the body of Christ—a struggle between individual liberties and communal values. On the fourth Sunday, the apostle examines the problem of eating food sacrificed to false idols—demonstrating how our choices may present temptations and stumbling blocks for others. On the sixth Sunday, the apostle addresses the importance of spiritual discipline in the exercise of faith—a familiar challenge in an age of excess and distraction, and a fitting theme as the season of Lent approaches.

As you travel through this Time after the Epiphany, you may find a variety of ways to "connect the dots"—both *among* the readings appointed for each Sunday (synchronically, or at the same time) and *across* the readings in a given span of weeks (diachronically, or through time). Indeed, this is a valuable homiletical and liturgical strategy in every time and season of the Christian year: seeking resonance among the weekly readings *and* looking for the threads that hold the weeks together, like beads on a string.

Making such connections will help us to order our steps, days, and lives according to God's word—in Ordinary Time and beyond.

Seasonal/Repeating Resources

These resources are intended for regular use throughout the Time after the Epiphany.

CONFESSION AND PARDON

The confession and pardon may be led from the baptismal font.

> Hear this good news of great joy for all:
> When Jesus was baptized,
> God's voice came down from heaven
> proclaiming, "This is my beloved Son
> in whom I am well pleased."

> Trusting in God's grace, let us confess our sin.

The confession may begin with a time of silence for personal prayer.

> **God of majesty and power,**
> **even as your voice shakes the wilderness**
> **and strips the forest bare, so it shakes us,**
> **stripping us of pretensions and illusions.**
> **In your presence we know without a doubt**
> **how we have wandered from your way,**
> **forgotten the sound of your voice,**
> **and failed to live into the gifts you have given us.**

> **Have mercy on us, Lord.**
> **Your word brings order to chaos, life to death.**
> **Speak to us again your promise of hope.**
> **Call to us again to live according to your justice.**
> **Call us by name to be your beloved children.**

Water may be poured or lifted from the baptismal font.

By joining God's family through baptism,
we share in Christ's own baptism.
We claim our place in God's beloved family.

In the name of Jesus Christ, God's beloved Son,
we are forgiven. **Thanks be to God.**

PRAYER FOR ILLUMINATION

The prayer for illumination is led from the lectern or pulpit.

Speak to us this day, O Lord,
with the breath of your Holy Spirit.
We know your voice is powerful enough
to shake the mountains
and to bring creation out of nothingness.
Today may it be loud enough
that we let go of our assumptions,
and quiet enough
that we hear your truth deep in our hearts;
in Jesus' name we pray. **Amen.**

THANKSGIVING FOR BAPTISM

The thanksgiving for baptism is led from the baptismal font.

*The introductory dialogue ("The Lord be with you . . .") may be sung
or spoken.*

O Lord our God, we are filled
with thanksgiving and praise,
blessing and honor and glory
for your gift of water, sustaining all of life.

We thank you for the gift of all water,
formed in the creation of the world.

We praise you for the gift of fresh water,
sustaining your people in the wilderness.

We bless you for the gift of healing water,
delivering Naaman from his illness.

We honor you for the gift of living water,
offered to the woman at the well.

We praise you for the gift of Spirit-filled water,
poured out on Jesus in his baptism at the Jordan
and poured out upon us in the church.

Through this water you have washed away our sins
and claimed us as your own in the body of Christ.
By your grace, continue to renew and restore us,
that we may live as your chosen people
in this world you love so much.

All thanks and praise
and blessing and honor
and glory be yours, O Lord,
this day and forevermore. **Amen.**

GREAT THANKSGIVING

The Great Thanksgiving is led from the Communion table.

*The introductory dialogue ("The Lord be with you . . .") may be sung
or spoken.*

We praise you, O God,
for all that you have done for us.
You created this world and all that is in it.
You made us as human beings in your own image.
You called us to live in community with you.
Even when we turned away from you,
you never withheld your love from us.

Therefore we sing our thanks and praise:

The Sanctus ("Holy, holy, holy . . .") may be sung or spoken.

Thank you, Lord, for Jesus Christ,
your Son and our Savior.
He lived a life of obedience to you,
showing us how to love one another.
He felt our joys and sorrows.
He kept company with those
who were considered unclean and unworthy.
Put to death by those he loved,
he rose again that we might have new life.

The words of institution are included here, if not elsewhere, while the bread and cup are lifted (but not broken/poured).

> We celebrate this meal
> as an offering of thanks and praise.
> In the breaking of this bread
> and the sharing of this cup,
> we give ourselves to you.

A memorial acclamation ("Christ has died . . .") may be sung or spoken.

> Lord God, pour out your Holy Spirit
> upon the bread and the cup
> and all who gather at this table.
> Make us one in your Spirit
> as we go forth into the world.
>
> Fill us with gratitude and wonder,
> justice and mercy, generosity and joy.
> Keep us faithful in following you—
> showing and sharing the love and peace
> that we have come to know in Christ,
> until he comes again in glory to reign.

A Trinitarian doxology and Great Amen may be sung or spoken.

PRAYER AFTER COMMUNION

The prayer after Communion is led from the Communion table.

> God of grace, we give you thanks
> for the meal we have shared
> in your beloved community.
> As we have received the bread and cup
> through the gift of your grace,
> send us forth in your Spirit
> to share these gifts with others,
> that they too may know and trust
> your presence, power, and love;
> through Jesus Christ our Lord. **Amen.**

PRAYER OF THANKSGIVING

The prayer of thanksgiving may be led from the Communion table.

Loving God, you are the source
of all goodness and mercy.
We praise you for your providence,
nurturing and sustaining all of life.
We thank you for your grace,
forgiving and delivering us from evil.
We bless you for your love,
binding us together in community.
By your Holy Spirit, fill us with gratitude,
that in your providence, grace, and love,
we may share these gifts with others;
in the name of Jesus Christ our Lord. **Amen.**

BLESSING

The blessing and charge may be led from the doors of the church.

Beloved people,
know that you are blessed
with the love of God,
the grace of Jesus Christ,
and the communion of the Holy Spirit,
now and always. **Alleluia!**

Baptism of the Lord

January 7–13

Genesis 1:1–5   Acts 19:1–7
Psalm 29   Mark 1:4–11

OPENING SENTENCES

> The voice of the Lord is over the waters;
> **the God of glory thunders,**
> **the Lord, over mighty waters.**
>
> The voice of the Lord is powerful;
> **the voice of the Lord is full of majesty.**
>
> And a voice came from heaven:
> **"You are my Son, the Beloved;**
> **with you I am well pleased."**

PRAYER OF THE DAY

> We are here, O God, listening for your voice.
> Silence in us any voice but yours,
> that we may be transformed this day in worship.
> Speak your voice into our hearts,
> our minds, our bones,
> so we will hear it in our very being. **Amen.**

INVITATION TO DISCIPLESHIP

The invitation to discipleship may be led from the baptismal font.

> God's voice is calling your name,
> calling you beloved.
> Are you ready to respond?
>
> You are invited to join in this life of faith,
> to claim your place in God's family through baptism.
> There is room for you here.
> Come, be beloved.
> Share beloved-ness with the world.

PRAYERS OF INTERCESSION

The prayers of intercession may be led from the midst of the congregation.

Holy God,
your voice spoke into the void and created the universe.
Your voice breaks the cedars and shakes the mountains.
Your voice calls out "Beloved" even today.

For the way you speak grace and mercy
into our lives and into our worlds,
we give you thanks.
Help us to listen for the echoes of your beloved cry
as we move through your good creation,
that we may hear our call to be caretakers and protectors
of what you have made and called good.

When you speak challenge and justice into the world,
we seek your courage.
May we never be afraid to work
for the reconciliation of the world.
May we always strive to be
on the side of your justice and shalom,
especially for the persecuted,
the oppressed, and the downtrodden.

Hear our prayers for your world . . .

Particular prayers may be offered.

Speak your word of comfort to those
facing illness, hospitalization, worry, and grief.
Call us into the stillness of your voice
so that we may hear your whispers of love and comfort
and be your presence in the lives of those
who feel alone, afraid, and discouraged.

Hear our prayers for loved ones . . .

Particular prayers may be offered.

Your voice causes the oaks to whirl
and strips the forest bare;
in your temple our voices cry, "Glory!"
You, O Lord, sit enthroned over the flood;
you sit enthroned as ruler forever.
Give strength to your people!
Bless your people with peace!

With boldness,
we ask you to hear our voices as we pray. **Amen.**

INVITATION TO OFFERING

The invitation to offering may be led from the Communion table.

God spoke this very world into being
and calls us today, declaring us and the world beloved.
Let us bring an offering of our very selves.
May our gifts of time, talent, and treasure glorify God
and serve God's children in the world.

INVITATION TO THE TABLE

The invitation to the table is led from the Communion table.

Perhaps you remember a time
when you've heard God's voice.
Maybe you hear it often.
Perhaps you have no memory of God speaking.
Whatever your experience has been, this is the place
where all of our experiences are brought together.
In this community,
we share our different experiences of faith,
offering support along the way.
At this table, God call us.
At this table, God feeds us.
At this table, there is a place set for you.
Yes, you.

Come to this table if you hear the call.
Come even if you're terrified to hear the call.
Come to this table,
because you are God's beloved child
and you are welcome here.

CHARGE

The blessing and charge may be led from the doors of the church.

You are God's beloved child.
Each of you. All of you.
Go and live your life in a way that invites others
to hear God's voice calling them beloved too.
Go and believe that every person you meet
is beloved by God and worthy of your care and attention.
Go and create beloved community
so the world may know they are loved and live accordingly.
Amen. *or* **Thanks be to God.**

Second Sunday after the Epiphany

January 14–20

1 Samuel 3:1–10 (11–20)   1 Corinthians 6:12–20
Psalm 139:1–6, 13–18   John 1:43–51

OPENING SENTENCES

O Lord, you have searched me and known me.
You know when I sit down and when I rise up;
you discern my thoughts from far away.

You search out my path and my lying down,
and are acquainted with all my ways.
Even before a word is on my tongue,
O Lord, you know it completely.

PRAYER OF THE DAY

O Lord, you have searched us and you know us.
Where could we go from your Spirit?
Or where could we flee from your presence?
If we were to catch a ride on the wings of the morning
and settle at the farthest limits of the sea,
even there your hand would lead us,
and your right hand would hold us fast.
Such knowledge is too wonderful for us, O God.
We can barely grasp the idea of it.
We are here to give you all of our praise
and all of our questions
and all of our doubts
and all of our hopes.
Gather us in,
surrounding us with your presence on all sides
as we worship you this day in joy. **Amen.**

INVITATION TO DISCIPLESHIP

The invitation to discipleship may be led from the baptismal font.

"Follow me."
Jesus invited his disciples to join him with a simple invitation.
"Follow me."
There were no strings attached.
They easily could not have followed him.
There was no threat of condemnation—only invitation.
"Come and see" was the invitation
the disciples extended to others.
No arguments, no conditions, no threat.
"Come and see."

You too are invited.
Come and see.
Join us, an imperfect gathering of beloved children of God
seeking to follow Jesus.
Come and see.

PRAYERS OF INTERCESSION

The prayers of intercession may be led from the midst of the congregation.

Speak, Lord; your servants are listening.
Even before words form on our tongues,
you know them.
And we rest in that assurance as we seek you,
as we are bold enough to voice our prayers,
our hopes, our worries, and our desires before you now.

For the gift of this day you have made,
we are thankful.
As the seasons change, and the earth spins,
and our lives unfold in ever-changing ways,
we are grateful for your abiding presence.

There is no place we could go
where you are not already there.
Help us to see glimpses of you
in war zones, in rubble,
in hospital wards, in halls of power,
in tent encampments, and in sleepless nights.
We pray for the wounded and hurting and worried and lonely.
Speak your word of peace in the hurting places.

Quiet the noise of our busy lives,
that we might rest in your presence
and tune our hearts to listen for your call.
Speak your still, small voice into our lives.
Speak, Lord. Your servants are listening. **Amen.**

INVITATION TO OFFERING

The invitation to offering may be led from the Communion table.

Jesus has invited us to follow him,
to come and see what God is doing in the world.

As our offering is received this morning,
let us give of our time, our talents, and our treasure,
that we may live into our calling
and participate in God's work and witness in the world.
Speak, Lord. We are listening.

INVITATION TO THE TABLE

The invitation to the table is led from the Communion table.

Come to the table.
Come and see that the Lord is good.
Come and be fed with the bread of life
and the cup of salvation.

Come and see how God's mystery
makes space for each one of us at this table.
Come and see that the Lord is good.

CHARGE

The blessing and charge may be led from the doors of the church.

Come and see.
God's call to you is not coercive or demanding.
It is a simple invitation to have our eyes,
our ears, our hearts, and our minds open
to look for God's presence in our world.
Go and live lives of invitation.
Go and be the people who welcome others,
that they may hear God's invitation for themselves.
God is calling you.
Answer the call.
Amen. *or* **Thanks be to God.**

Third Sunday after the Epiphany

January 21–27

Jonah 3:1–5, 10   1 Corinthians 7:29–31
Psalm 62:5–12   Mark 1:14–20

OPENING SENTENCES

> Nets and fishes,
> work and profits,
> occupy our days.
> **You call us: "Follow me."**
>
> Safety and comfort,
> a life well-established,
> you ask us to leave.
> **You call us: "Follow me."**
>
> So we leave all we know,
> we trust your promise,
> we are here to hear the good news:
> **"The time is fulfilled,**
> **God's reign is near."**
> **Good news indeed! Alleluia!**

PRAYER OF THE DAY

> O God, you call us
> to drop our nets,
> to cast our nets into the unknown.
> We are scared but want to trust.
> Help us to bear good news,
> help us to build a kingdom of justice,
> and help us be the fulfillment of peace
> in the universe. **Amen.**

INVITATION TO DISCIPLESHIP

The invitation to discipleship may be led from the baptismal font.

Jesus comes to us,
and asks us to follow him
just as we are—
with gifts and attachments,
worries and fears.

Drop your nets and follow him!
Repent!
Good news awaits!

PRAYERS OF INTERCESSION

The prayers of intercession may be led from the midst of the congregation.

In these troubling times,
full of violence and political turmoil,
our souls wait in silence.

In the depths of despair,
as we see kindness fizzle out,
our souls wait in silence.

In the loneliness we feel
in a world of perfect pictures and smiles,
our souls wait in silence.

When we don't know what else to do
to change the world,
our souls wait in silence.

Help us, O God,
to trust in you at all times.
Give us the refuge of hope.
Give us the strength of a rock.
Engrave in our hearts the message
that power belongs to you alone,
that steadfast love is yours,
that you are holding us near,
that you are our salvation. **Amen.**

INVITATION TO OFFERING

The invitation to offering may be led from the Communion table.

The world as we know it is passing away.

Trusting in the promise of life abundant,
let us share our lives and prayers,
our gifts and our hopes
with the one who is turning the world around.

INVITATION TO THE TABLE

The invitation to the table is led from the Communion table.

Jesus invites us to witness a new world
and to be fishers of people—
but not without sustenance,
nourishment for the work we have ahead.

God has prepared a meal for us.
Let us feast on love!

CHARGE

The blessing and charge may be led from the doors of the church.

Drop everything you are doing and follow Jesus!
Believe the good news!
The kingdom of God is near!
Amen. *or* **Thanks be to God.**

Fourth Sunday after the Epiphany

January 28—February 3

Deuteronomy 18:15–20   1 Corinthians 8:1–13
Psalm 111   Mark 1:21–28

OPENING SENTENCES

I am your God;
I promise never to leave you.
We are your people;
we are not afraid.

You are my people;
I will always be just and true.
You are our God;
we lift our hearts to you.

PRAYER OF THE DAY

God, you are renowned
for your wonderful deeds of kindness.
Your love elevates us.
Jesus, you do marvelous acts
that are not easy to understand,
making a path through pain,
repurposing the cross for salvation.
Spirit, open a portion of God's wisdom
to our hearts, and inspire us
to continue the marvelous works
of Jesus in the world. **Amen.**

INVITATION TO DISCIPLESHIP

The invitation to discipleship may be led from the baptismal font.

God doesn't remain silent
in the cacophony of injustice.
God promised to send prophets,
and God is no oath breaker.
Today, God calls you to be a prophet
who speaks wisdom and truth,
to call out the false gods of greed and racism,
and other false idols that separate us.

The Word of God burns in your soul.
Do not let fear hold you.
Let God speak through you.

PRAYERS OF INTERCESSION

The prayers of intercession may be led from the midst of the congregation.

God of knowledge and wisdom,
you know our prayers better than we do.
So guide our words and thoughts
as we entrust them to your wisdom.
Hear us as we pray.

For humility,
that we would not boast of our strengths
but use them to carry the weak;
that we would be strong enough
to admit our weakness
and to seek the strength of others.

For the humbling of nations,
that they might not lord power over people
like false gods,
but like you, Almighty God,
be ready to serve the people,
ready to leave the ninety-nine for the one.

For our neighborhoods,
that they would not be clusters of sameness
through the practice of exclusion,
but by your wisdom and truth
offer inclusion to all.

For knowledge of you,
a knowledge that keeps us open to awe,
a knowledge that humbles us to listen
to all our siblings,
to the sibling beings of all living things,
and to the ancient knowledge and wisdom
of plants and trees and dirt.

Yes, help us to listen respectfully
to the entire family of beings on this earth. **Amen.**

INVITATION TO OFFERING

The invitation to offering may be led from the Communion table.

Nothing we currently have
began with us or should end with us.
Currency is like currents of water.
The rain comes and waters the earth,
helping flowers bear fruit;
then it returns to the heavens,
a circle of giving and receiving
made by God's wisdom.

Let us release everything
back into God's economy.

INVITATION TO THE TABLE

The invitation to the table is led from the Communion table.

This is the table of the Lord.
The Lord has invited everyone.
There is no one so strong and good
that they don't need the bread of Christ.
There is no one so weak and broken
that they don't deserve the blood of Christ.

You may think of yourself as disqualified or overqualified.
But Jesus doesn't think so.
Come. There is a seat and a meal for you.

CHARGE

The blessing and charge may be led from the doors of the church.

You have been nourished by the bread of Christ.
You have been anointed by the Holy Spirit.
God's living Word lives in you.
God's holy Word cleanses you.
Go and proclaim God's Word—
in dance, in protest, in art,
in song, in listening, in all that you do.
Amen. *or* **Thanks be to God.**

Fifth Sunday after the Epiphany

February 4–10

Isaiah 40:21–31
Psalm 147:1–11, 20c

1 Corinthians 9:16–23
Mark 1:29–39

OPENING SENTENCES

> Who is like our God, who names the stars?
> **Great is our God.**
> **Give God the praise.**
>
> Who is like our God, who knows our names?
> **Gracious is our God.**
> **Give God our love.**

PRAYER OF THE DAY

> Amazing God,
> you created this marvelous earth,
> made to sustain all living things,
> and made it beautiful,
> delighting our senses.
> Beautiful Jesus,
> you joined us on earth.
> Although we ruined ourselves
> through our arrogance and violence,
> you taught us with parables and healing
> how to restore relationship with God.
> Powerful Holy Spirit,
> give us the power and love of Jesus
> to keep walking the good walk
> and doing our part
> in restoring this beautiful world. **Amen.**

INVITATION TO DISCIPLESHIP

The invitation to discipleship may be led from the baptismal font.

There are many in this world
hungry and broken and tired,
like us.
We are not sent as saviors,
but as ones who also need rescuing.
We meet Jesus as we do the work of Jesus.
We are healed by those we heal.
We are mended by those we mend.

We invite you to join us in this work.
Be ready to be all things to all people,
so you might find yourself.
This is the way of Jesus.

PRAYERS OF INTERCESSION

The prayers of intercession may be led from the midst of the congregation.

God, you never tire,
keeping watch over creation.
We, on the other hand,
get tired and need rest.
We are weak, so we pray.
We need your help.

We pray for our church . . .
that we can be the church for all people,
especially for those
who don't have a place in this world.
In your church may they find a home,
a place where they find new strength,
where they find rest.

We pray for our world . . .
There is sickness and exhaustion
in our bodies and in our governments.
The strong think they can do anything
and get away with it.
Shatter the pride of the strong,
and to the weak reveal their strength.

Care for us tenderly.
We are only mortals,
gone by the time the sun rises tomorrow.
Your breath could blow us away.
But breathe on us as you breathed
into the lungs of the first human.
Let it be the breath of new life. **Amen.**

INVITATION TO OFFERING

The invitation to offering may be led from the Communion table.

God has never given up on us—
even when we give up on ourselves,
even when we give up on our siblings
and on the world.
God breathes away the dross
and breathes into us stupendous power.

Let that powerful grace
flow through us and in us.
Let that grace flow out as generosity,
for our generosity can be inspiration
to those on the verge of quitting,
giving them power not to quit.

INVITATION TO THE TABLE

The invitation to the table is led from the Communion table.

Jesus wants to feed our souls
and heal our bodies
so the sick can walk
and those who walk can run.
With Jesus there is time for the healing of everyone.
There is no need to push others away.
We are not fighting for a limited resource.

Come, confident that you have a place,
and carry others with you.
They too have a place.

CHARGE

The blessing and charge may be led from the doors of the church.

> Can you contain yourself
> when you have heard the great news
> that God is for us and not against us?
> Then don't try to contain it.
> Go out into your world
> and share this great news
> with all the people in your life.
> They will want to know who sent you
> with this great news that they are not alone.
> **Amen.** *or* **Thanks be to God.**

Sixth Sunday after the Epiphany

February 11–17, if before Transfiguration

2 Kings 5:1–14
Psalm 30

1 Corinthians 9:24–27
Mark 1:40–45

OPENING SENTENCES

Weeping may linger for the night,
but joy comes with the morning.

The Lord will turn our mourning into dancing;
God will remove our sorrow and clothe us with joy.

Praise the Lord, O my soul, and do not be silent;
Give thanks to the Lord our God forever.

PRAYER OF THE DAY

O Lord our God,
your word is life and healing,
and your compassion is great.
As you worked through Elisha and Jesus
to welcome outcasts and heal disease,
wash away our suffering and shame,
that we may rejoice and give you praise;
through Jesus Christ our Savior. **Amen.**

INVITATION TO DISCIPLESHIP

The invitation to discipleship may be led from the baptismal font.

The call to discipleship is not a difficult command.
Jesus simply says:
Come to me, believe in me,
and I will make all things new.

Are you ready to take the next steps in faith?
We are eager to walk beside you.

PRAYERS OF INTERCESSION

The prayers of intercession may be led from the midst of the congregation.

To you, O Lord, we cry;
to you we make our supplication:
O Lord our helper, **be gracious to us.**

Give wisdom to the leaders of nations,
that they may seek your way.
O Lord our helper, **be gracious to us.**

Replace the weapons of war
with instruments of healing and peace.
O Lord our helper, **be gracious to us.**

Give comfort to those who sit in sorrow,
restoring their courage and joy.
O Lord our helper, **be gracious to us.**

Be near to all who suffer,
reaching out to them with compassion.
O Lord our helper, **be gracious to us.**

Draw us up from the depths, O God,
that we may praise your faithfulness
and give thanks to your holy name;
through Jesus Christ our Lord. **Amen.**

INVITATION TO OFFERING

The invitation to offering may be led from the Communion table.

Let us devote ourselves to God's work,
sharing freely with others,
exercising discipline and self-control,
and seeking the imperishable prize
of God's eternal realm.

With generosity and gladness,
let us offer our gifts and lives to God.

INVITATION TO THE TABLE

The invitation to the table is led from the Communion table.

This is the feast of redemption,
a banquet of life made new.
Put aside your sackcloth and ashes;
put on a garment of joy.
Here we will sing with gladness
and dance with thanksgiving.

Come to the table of the Lord.

CHARGE

The blessing and charge may be led from the doors of the church.

Be faithful in simple things,
trusting that the grace of God
will make you holy and whole.
Amen. *or* **Thanks be to God.**

Seventh Sunday after the Epiphany

February 18–24, if before Transfiguration

Isaiah 43:18–25   2 Corinthians 1:18–22
Psalm 41   Mark 2:1–12

OPENING SENTENCES

> O people, God has formed you
> and God loves you.
> **God has made rivers in the desert**
> **and has given water in the wilderness.**
>
> Even now, in our midst, God is doing a new thing—
> do you perceive it?
> **We will seek it, yearn for it,**
> **so that we might declare God's praise.**

PRAYER OF THE DAY

> O God of patient presence,
> though we sometimes grow weary of seeking you,
> you never tire of reaching out to us.
> Enliven in us an eagerness
> not only to enjoy your presence for ourselves
> but also, through all that we say and do,
> to break down barriers
> that prevent others from seeking you—
> barriers that we so often build
> when we cling too tightly
> to previous understandings
> of who you are and how you love.
> Stir in us a joyful curiosity
> for all of the ways you might surprise us,
> so that we might perceive the numerous ways
> you are reaching out to those
> in need of your abundant mercy,
> through Jesus Christ,
> your living, exuberant "Yes!" **Amen.**

INVITATION TO DISCIPLESHIP

The invitation to discipleship may be led from the baptismal font.

> Like the faithful friends
> who brought their sick loved one to Jesus,
> we are called to tear down old structures
> in pursuit of the new thing that God is doing,
> that all those in need of healing and hope
> might seek God and be found.
>
> In what ways are you being called to act faithfully,
> so that those in need of it might experience God's presence?

PRAYERS OF INTERCESSION

The prayers of intercession may be led from the midst of the congregation.

> O God, let us not become weary
> in coming to you
> with everything that is on our hearts.
> Embolden us to call on you,
> even as you reach out to us.
>
> O God, we lift up to you the poor,
> struggling to make ends meet,
> hungry and thirsty in both body and spirit,
> longing for stability.
> God, may your abundance spring forth,
> **and help us to perceive it.**
>
> O God, we lift up to you the sick,
> facing illnesses seen and unseen,
> weary in both body and spirit,
> yearning for relief.
> God, may your healing spring forth,
> **and help us to perceive it.**
>
> O God, we lift up to you the betrayed,
> lamenting loss of trust,
> seeking justice,
> confronting broken systems.
> God, may your faithfulness spring forth,
> **and help us to perceive it.**

O God, we lift up to you the wilderness,
reeling from our overuse,
drying out or flooding,
losing habitat and home.
God, may your restoration spring forth,
and help us to perceive it.

O God, who upholds us
and sets us in your presence,
you continue to surprise us by doing new things.
Make your presence evident to us
in every situation,
even as we lift our prayers to you,
through Jesus Christ,
in the power of the Holy Spirit. **Amen.**

INVITATION TO OFFERING

The invitation to offering may be led from the Communion table.

The God who makes rivers in the desert—
who is doing a new thing,
who does not grow weary in responding to us—
that God provides what we need for each day.

In gratitude, let us give of ourselves
in support of God's work in the world.

INVITATION TO THE TABLE

The invitation to the table is led from the Communion table.

God, who gives water in the wilderness,
has set a table for us—
a table of grace,
a table of forgiveness,
a table of remembrance.

Let all who are thirsty come.

CHARGE

The blessing and charge may be led from the doors of the church.

As surely as God is faithful,
we have been given God's Spirit in our hearts.
May we go out with eagerness
for all that God is doing,
seeking to perceive God's new thing
with awe and great rejoicing.
Amen. *or* **Thanks be to God.**

Eighth Sunday after the Epiphany

February 25–29, if before Transfiguration

Hosea 2:14–20   2 Corinthians 3:1–6
Psalm 103:1–13, 22   Mark 2:13–22

OPENING SENTENCES

> O my whole being,
> all that is within me:
> **Bless God's holy name.**
>
> Come, bless the Holy One with me,
> for as high as the heavens are above the earth,
> **so great is God's steadfast love**
> **toward those fear God.**

PRAYER OF THE DAY

> Merciful God,
> your steadfast love and faithfulness
> will not let you turn from us.
> You speak tenderly to us
> and to all your creation,
> longing for us to offer back to you
> a love letter, written on our hearts.
> O God, make us ministers of a new covenant,
> written not with ink
> but with your living, lively Spirit,
> who calls us to follow you
> with our whole selves
> in compassionate care for all your children
> and all creation.
> Help us to recognize those who are sick among us
> and the sickness within ourselves.
> And enable us to craft, with you,
> a new healing—holy and whole,
> through the power of that same Spirit. **Amen.**

INVITATION TO DISCIPLESHIP

The invitation to discipleship may be led from the baptismal font.

God calls to us tenderly,
inviting us to follow
into a new covenant of generous love.

Will we become ministers of this new covenant,
writing our love not only with words
but with all that we do and all that we are?

PRAYERS OF INTERCESSION

The prayers of intercession may be led from the midst of the congregation.

O God, you have made your ways known to us
across time and space;
stories abound of your loving care.
Help us not to forget your compassion
for all of your children,
but rather, in this moment,
encourage us to approach you with confidence,
trusting you with all that weighs heavy on our hearts.

God, we entrust to you
those stricken by all kinds of disease,
who ache in body and spirit,
and sorrow in beds and in silence.
**Grant to them, O blessed one,
caring hands and compassionate hearts,
vessels of your healing.**

God, we entrust to you
those in the pit of despair,
who witness the destruction of your creation
and the debasing of your children.
**Grant to them, O blessed one,
willing kindred spirits that seek repair,
and perseverance for the journey.**

God, we entrust to you
those longing for good things,
who hunger for food and for justice
and yearn for water and for peace.
**Grant to them, O blessed one,
rest amid their restlessness,
and companions in their questing.**

God, we entrust to you
those cast out and despised,
who desire belonging and stability
and seek a new home or a recognition of new identity.
**Grant to them, O blessed one,
a community that knows them,
welcomes them, loves them.**

O God, let our souls not forget all you have provided:
you forgive all iniquity,
you heal our diseases,
you redeem life from the Pit,
you crown us with steadfast love and mercy,
and you satisfy us with good as long as we live,
so that our youth is renewed like the eagle's.
O God, may we participate
in your answer to our prayers,
even as we wait with eagerness
for your redemption of this whole world;
through Jesus Christ we pray. **Amen.**

INVITATION TO OFFERING

The invitation to offering may be led from the Communion table.

We have confidence through Christ toward God—
not that we bring anything of ourselves,
but that God has made us qualified
and has equipped us to participate in Christ's ministry.

Secure in that knowledge,
let us give from what God has provided.

INVITATION TO THE TABLE

The invitation to the table is led from the Communion table.

This is God's table,
where all are invited—
sinner and saint,
confident and questioning,
and many who are all the above and more.
Here there is a clean cup,
fresh bread,
and a new covenant
for all of us to share.

All has been made ready;
come, let us partake of the feast.

CHARGE

The blessing and charge may be led from the doors of the church.

With all that you are,
show that you are a love letter of Christ,
written not with ink
but with the Spirit of the living God.
Amen. *or* **Thanks be to God.**

Ninth Sunday after the Epiphany

If Transfiguration is not observed on the Sunday before Lent begins

Deuteronomy 5:12–15   2 Corinthians 4:5–12
Psalm 81:1–10   Mark 2:23–3:6

OPENING SENTENCES

> Sing aloud to God our strength;
> shout for joy to the God of Jacob.
> **Raise a song; sound the tambourine;**
> **strum the sweet lyre with the harp.**
>
> Blow the trumpet at the new moon,
> at the full moon, on our festal day.
> **For our God, who brought the people out of Egypt,**
> **has relieved our shoulders of burdens**
> **and created this Sabbath day of rest for all.**

PRAYER OF THE DAY

> O author and sustainer of Sabbath,
> you did not create us to work but to be.
> You brought your people Israel
> out of bondage in Egypt,
> and you invite us into your freedom today.
> Let us not look to ability or lack of ability—
> our own or that of others—
> as a measure of dignity or worth.
> Rather, in resting from our restlessness,
> let us become wide open
> to receive the life you would give us,
> that we might experience your glory
> in everyone we meet
> and in ourselves too.
> All this we pray through Jesus Christ,
> whose death is at work in us
> to bring about life abundant. **Amen.**

INVITATION TO DISCIPLESHIP

The invitation to discipleship may be led from the baptismal font.

Through this Sabbath day,
when lights are dimmed and activities slowed,
the God who said, "Light will shine out of darkness,"
has shone in our hearts,
giving us a glimpse of the knowledge of God's glory
in the face of Jesus Christ,
who shines in every face we encounter.

Will you hold beloved darkness close—
the mysterious restoration birthed by rest and sleep?
In this time of Sabbath, you are invited
to let every crack and crevice
be restored with God's shimmering love,
that you might shine in this world of shadows.

PRAYERS OF INTERCESSION

The prayers of intercession may be led from the midst of the congregation.

Where there are ellipses (. . .), leaders should provide ample time for worshipers to consider names and speak or cry them aloud, or to reflect on them in silence.

When the leader says, "We stretch out our hands to you," worshipers may be invited to extend their own hands, lift their heads, contemplate an appropriate image, or practice some other form of embodied prayer.

O God of compassion,
our companion on the way,
Lord of the Sabbath in all its wholeness,
you invite us to come to you,
to bring our humanity at full stretch before you—
every moment of rejoicing
and each hour of sorrow,
our simmering anger,
and our hushed silence.
So we come to you now,
trusting that you hear us,
confident in your care.

O God,
who brought your people out of Egypt,
liberate those who are languishing
in oppressive, abusive, and unjust situations.
We speak their names to you now . . .
O God, we stretch out our hands to you;
be merciful to us.

O Christ,
whose disciples picked grain from the fields,
nourish all those who are hungry
and in need of food and the basics of life.
We speak their names to you now . . .
O God, we stretch out our hands to you;
be merciful to us.

O Great Physician,
who restored a man with a withered hand,
bring swift healing to those who are suffering
from a variety of ailments.
We speak their names to you now . . .
O God, we stretch out our hands to you;
be merciful to us.

O Lord of the Sabbath,
relieve the burdens of all those who are crushed
under the weight of stress and anxiety,
loneliness and despair.
We speak their names to you now . . .
O God, we stretch out our hands to you;
be merciful to us.

O lover of all humankind,
bring peace to all those who are caught
in situations of strife, war, and violence—
a holistic peace,
not just the absence of conflict,
but the presence of humane actions
and just decisions.
We speak their names to you now . . .
O God, we stretch out our hands to you;
be merciful to us.

O God,
we are afflicted in every way but not crushed,
perplexed but not driven to despair,
persecuted but not forsaken,
struck down but not destroyed.
We carry around in our bodies the death of Jesus,
so that the life of Jesus may also be made visible.
May we also carry these prayers that we have offered,
so that the knowledge of your glory may be made evident;
through Jesus Christ, Lord of the Sabbath, we pray. **Amen.**

(The language of "humanity at full stretch" derives from the work of liturgical theologian Don E. Saliers.)

INVITATION TO OFFERING

The invitation to offering may be led from the Communion table.

Like clay jars,
beautiful vessels made to receive,
we have been filled with the goodness of God.

With gratitude, let us pour out what we are able,
that God's goodness might be shared with all.

INVITATION TO THE TABLE

The invitation to the table is led from the Communion table.

Our God knows when we are hungry—
for food and companionship,
for freedom and justice,
for forgiveness and peace.
With the grain of the fields,
the fruit of the vine,
and the coursing waters,
God has provided all that is needed for this table of grace.

Come, stretch out your hand;
come, open your hearts;
come, renew your spirits.

CHARGE

The blessing and charge may be led from the doors of the church.

As we carry around Jesus' death,
that his life might be visible in our bodies,
let us stretch ourselves out
and open ourselves up
to receive the goodness God has for us,
that we might share God's glory with all we meet.
Amen. *or* **Thanks be to God.**

Transfiguration Sunday

Sunday before Lent begins

2 Kings 2:1–12
Psalm 50:1–6

2 Corinthians 4:3–6
Mark 9:2–9

OPENING SENTENCES

"Gather to me my faithful ones,"
says our righteous and beautiful God.
God speaks and summons the earth
from the rising of the sun to its setting.

Our God comes and does not keep silent;
God comes in the tempest and fire,
in the stillness and the silence.

Let us still our hearts to listen.
Come, let us worship God.

PRAYER OF THE DAY

O deep well of holy mystery,
in seeking you and embracing you
we discover that we are found by you,
and we recognize that there is more to you
than our hearts and minds could ever hold.
Though we long for your presence,
we too often experience an aching absence,
and this terrifies us.
Let us not hold on to you
or cling too tightly to our ideas of who you are;
instead, may we gladly follow you,
knowing that you are a living God
who calls us into your world
and into relationship
with all who seek your loving embrace.
All this we ask through your Holy Spirit,
rushing like a wild wind. **Amen.**

INVITATION TO DISCIPLESHIP

The invitation to discipleship may be led from the baptismal font.

> Beloved children of a loving God,
> we follow one who dazzles us and baffles us,
> who is both mystery and deep meaning.
>
> When we cry out in terror and sorrow,
> will we trust that God hears us?
> When we feel keenly the sense of God's absence,
> will we trust that God loves us?
> When we experience a sudden transformation
> in who we thought we knew God was,
> will we trust that God will find us again and again?

PRAYERS OF INTERCESSION

The prayers of intercession may be led from the midst of the congregation.

Where there are ellipses (. . .), leaders should provide ample time for worshipers to consider names, places, or events and speak them aloud, or to reflect on them in silence.

When the leader says, "God of compassion," worshipers may be invited to extend their own hands, lift their heads, contemplate an appropriate image, or practice some other form of embodied prayer.

> O Abyss of Kindness,
> you are a never-ending source
> of care and compassion.
> When we cry to you
> in terror and sorrow,
> in joy and hope,
> you respond:
> **"You are my children, my beloved;**
> **I am listening."**
>
> God, we bring to you now
> the terrors and sorrows,
> the joys and hopes
> that emerge from the cries of our global community . . .
> God of compassion,
> **hear our prayers.**

God, we bring to you now
the terrors and sorrows,
the joys and hopes
that emerge from the cries of the nation in which we live . . .
God of compassion,
hear our prayers.

God, we bring to you now
the terrors and sorrows,
the joys and hopes
that emerge from the cries of the city in which we dwell . . .
God of compassion,
hear our prayers.

God, we bring to you now
the terrors and sorrows,
the joys and hopes
that emerge from the cries of the people within our homes . . .
God of compassion,
hear our prayers.

God, we bring to you now
the terrors and sorrows,
the joys and hopes
that emerge from the cries within our own hearts . . .
God of compassion,
hear our prayers.

Unveil yourself to us, O God,
that we might bask in your presence
and rest in your care.
May the compassion we receive from you
stir us toward compassion for all your creation.
This we pray through Jesus Christ. **Amen.**

("Abyss of Kindness" was a phrase often used by Brother Roger of Taizé.)

INVITATION TO OFFERING

The invitation to offering may be led from the Communion table.

Like Elisha inheriting a double share
of his mentor's spirit,
like the disciples astonished
by Jesus' dazzling appearance,
we have been given great gifts
through the glory of God.

Let us not try to hide them away,
but instead let us share them,
that all may experience the goodness of God.

INVITATION TO THE TABLE

The invitation to the table is led from the Communion table.

This table of grace and mystery
is both simple and complex.
The bread, the cup, the plates, the cloth—
these are materials so common to our daily life.
Yet God transforms them
into nourishment for the long journey of faith,
the body and blood of Jesus Christ.

Come, beloved, in your simplicity
and in your complexity.
All of you is welcome;
all of us are welcome.

CHARGE

The blessing and charge may be led from the doors of the church.

May we, like Elisha,
so desire closeness to God
that we pledge never to leave God's side.
May we, like the disciples,
with fear and trembling,
be willing to experience the God we haven't yet known,
letting go of our preconceptions
even as we follow Jesus down the mountain
to serve a weary world.
Amen. *or* **Thanks be to God.**

SEASON OF LENT

Making Connections

The season of Lent consists of the forty days from Ash Wednesday to Holy Saturday. The six Sundays within this span of weeks are not numbered among the forty days of Lent, because each Sunday is a celebration of Christ's resurrection on the first day of the week. (For this reason, we refer to them as Sundays "in Lent" instead of Sundays "of Lent.") Throughout the history of the church, this penitential season has been a time of preparation for baptism, reconciliation with God and neighbor, the renewal of spiritual disciplines, and reflection on the mystery of Christ's dying and rising.

After Jesus was baptized by John in the Jordan River, Mark's Gospel tells us that "the Spirit immediately drove him out into the wilderness" (Mark 1:12). Mark continues: "He was in the wilderness forty days, tempted by Satan; and he was with the wild beasts; and the angels waited on him" (Mark 1:13). Linked with baptism, filled with spiritual challenges, yet surrounded and sustained by divine grace, Jesus' forty days in the wilderness set the pattern for the church's Lenten journey.

Year B of the Revised Common Lectionary provides opportunities to make connections with several notable "forty" stories during the Lenten season. On the first Sunday in Lent, God establishes a new covenant with Noah (Gen. 9:8–17) after forty days and nights of rain that washed away the sin of the earth. On the third Sunday, God presents the gift of the law at Mount Sinai (Exod. 20:1–17), where Moses spent forty days and nights. On the fourth Sunday, God provides a sign of death and life—like the cross of Jesus—to deliver the people from a plague of poisonous serpents (Num. 21:4–9) in the wilderness where they wandered for forty years.

As you journey through the forty days of Lent, consider how such stories might illuminate and inform your own time in the wilderness. With Jesus, reflect on how you are living out your baptismal calling, confronting spiritual challenges, and relying on God's grace. With Noah, remember God's covenant of grace, washing away sin and evil. With Moses, spend time in God's presence, devoting yourself to God's word. With the people of Israel, seek healing, deliverance, and reconciliation with God as you travel from captivity to freedom. Through preaching, liturgy, music, and the arts, help worshipers understand the connections among these and other theological themes and biblical stories, and how they guide our life of faith.

May these forty days of Lent equip and prepare you to celebrate new life in Christ during the fifty days of Easter. As Jesus said upon returning from the wilderness, "The time is fulfilled" (Mark 1:15).

Seasonal/Repeating Resources

These resources are intended for regular use throughout the season of Lent.

CONFESSION AND PARDON

The confession and pardon may be led from the baptismal font.

> In this time when so much is focused on outward spectacle,
> it is right that we take a detour to examine our inward life.
>
> Let us confess our sins before God and one another,
> first in silence, then aloud.

The confession may begin with a time of silence for personal prayer.

> **Holy One, you enter into our lives**
> **in ways we could not have expected.**
> **Sometimes, we confess, we think**
> **you are making a fool of yourself and us.**
> **We cannot see how your way can work, or be right,**
> **because it is so contrary to our ambition and understanding.**
> **Yet we shout our hosannas and sing our praises.**
>
> **Forgive us for projecting all our narrow worldly views on you**
> **and expecting you to live up to our standards.**
> **Forgive us for not trusting your way of peace.**
> **Take our palm branches and our lives,**
> **that we may learn to lay them down in your service,**
> **following your way even when we cannot understand.**
> **This we pray in the name of the one who made a parade**
> **with only a donkey and some children singing for your glory,**
> **Jesus the Christ.**

Water may be poured or lifted from the baptismal font.

Our "hosannas" are a cry for God to save us.
The good news is this: God hears our cries.
God forgives our sin.
God restores us.
Jesus the Christ, who came to save,
leads us on the path of peace.

In the name of Jesus Christ, we are forgiven.
Thanks be to God.

PRAYER FOR ILLUMINATION

The prayer for illumination is led from the lectern or pulpit.

Speak to us now, O Lord.
Guide us by your Word and Spirit
all along this Lenten journey.
Open our hearts and minds
to understand and follow
what you are saying to us
in the message of the Scriptures.
Empower us in these forty days
to live into your ways in the world;
through Jesus Christ we pray. **Amen.**

THANKSGIVING FOR BAPTISM

The thanksgiving for baptism is led from the baptismal font.

The introductory dialogue ("The Lord be with you . . .") may be sung or spoken.

Thank you, O God,
for the gift of our baptism—
the sign of your abundant mercy,
the seal of your steadfast love.

Through the grace of Jesus Christ
you wash away our iniquity
and cleanse us from our sin.
You create clean hearts for us
and renew our spirits within us.

By the power of your Holy Spirit,
restore to us the joy of salvation.
Strengthen and sustain us
in our willingness to serve you
now and in all days to come.

Open our lips, O Lord,
and we will declare your praise;
through Jesus Christ our Savior. **Amen.**

GREAT THANKSGIVING

The Great Thanksgiving is led from the Communion table.

The introductory dialogue ("The Lord be with you . . .") may be sung or spoken.

Holy One, we glorify your name.
You create the heavens and the earth.
You claim us as your people
and call us from slavery to freedom.
When we wander in the wilderness
you feed us with manna from heaven
and lead us home by your word.

Therefore we join the ancient song:

The Sanctus ("Holy, holy, holy . . .") may be sung or spoken.

Holy One, we glorify your name.
Into this world of suffering and sin
you send a Savior, Jesus Christ—
born to share our life,
living to teach your way,
following that way to death,
dying to rise again in glory,
rising to give life to all the world.

The words of institution are included here, if not elsewhere, while the bread and cup are lifted (but not broken/poured).

We offer our lives to your glory
as we share this feast of grace,
remembering the words of Jesus:
Unless a grain of wheat
falls to the earth and dies,
it remains just a single grain;
but if it dies, it bears much fruit.

A memorial acclamation ("Christ has died . . .") may be sung or spoken.

Holy One, we glorify your name.
Pour out your Holy Spirit, we pray,
upon the bread, the cup, your people,
that we may have communion with you
in the body and blood of Christ our Lord.
Guide us through these forty days,
through the mystery of cross and tomb,
and into the promise of eternal life.

Spirit, Savior, Sovereign God,
we glorify your name.

A Trinitarian doxology and Great Amen may be sung or spoken.

PRAYER AFTER COMMUNION

The prayer after Communion is led from the Communion table.

Holy One, we glorify your name—
for the bread of heaven
and the cup of blessing;
for the grace of Christ
and the power of the Spirit;
for the gift of faith
and the joy of service;
for the life of the world
and the hope of new creation.
Thanks and praise to you, O God;
through Jesus Christ our Lord. **Amen.**

PRAYER OF THANKSGIVING

The prayer of thanksgiving may be led from the Communion table.

We give you thanks and praise, O God,
for you are rich in mercy, sharing with us
the immeasurable riches of your grace.
By this grace you have saved us
through faith in Jesus Christ our Lord.
By the power of your Holy Spirit
equip us to be what you made us to be—
a people created for good works
as a way of life in Christ Jesus,
in whose holy name we pray. **Amen.**

BLESSING

The blessing and charge may be led from the doors of the church.

The blessing of God,
who so loves the world;
the blessing of Jesus,
who teaches us to love one another;
and the blessing of the Holy Spirit,
who brings love to birth,
be with you and with all. **Amen.**

The Alleluia in response to the blessing is traditionally omitted in Lent.

Ash Wednesday

Joel 2:1–2, 12–17
  or Isaiah 58:1–12
Psalm 51:1–17

2 Corinthians 5:20b–6:10
Matthew 6:1–6, 16–21

The liturgy for Ash Wednesday marks the beginning of Lent, a season of penitence and preparation for Easter. On Ash Wednesday we confront the hard realities of human finitude and failure, confessing our dependence on divine grace for salvation from sin and death.

The primary theological themes of Ash Wednesday include repentance from sin, renewal of spiritual disciplines, and reconciliation with God and neighbor. Distinctive elements of the liturgy are the invitation to observe a holy Lent, the litany of penitence (in combination with Psalm 51), and the imposition of ashes.

The resources that follow are intended to offer creativity, flexibility, and additional options for the church's celebration of Ash Wednesday. Selected texts may be incorporated into the liturgies provided in denominational service books, such as the Presbyterian Church (U.S.A.) *Book of Common Worship* (pp. 247–57). Or they may be used in combination with other materials, found in this book or elsewhere, to develop new liturgies for Ash Wednesday.

OPENING SENTENCES

The people are gathered;
elders and children
and even nursing infants are here.
We come with fasting,
with weeping,
and with sorrow.

We are here to change our hearts,
to return to you with our whole hearts.
We are here to worship you, O merciful one!

PRAYER OF THE DAY

With grace and compassion
you invite us to return to you.
Patient and full of faithful love,
you ask us to return to you.
Ready to forgive us,
you demand a fast from us.
You want our hearts and not our festivals,
our lives and not our empty promises.
Open our lips,
and we will praise you.
Guide us back to you;
we are ready. **Amen.**

INVITATION TO DISCIPLESHIP
AND INVITATION TO OBSERVE A HOLY LENT

The invitation to discipleship may be led from the baptismal font.

Death, dust, ashes—
transformed by fasting, repenting, returning to God;
nurtured by grace, compassion, forgiveness.
Empty promises turn into true sacrifices,
shallow rituals turn into acts of renewal,
shame and despair turn into assurance and hope,
all by the love of God,
through the love of God,
in the love of God.

This is a season to reflect on who we are
and whose we are,
to declutter our minds
from all that distracts us from love,
to rest from busyness
and recalibrate our compasses.

I invite you to observe a holy Lent—
to pray and fast,
to feed and clothe others,
to repent and to forgive,
to open ourselves to the possibility of a different world.
God will be with us every step of the way.

PRAYERS OF INTERCESSION

The prayers of intercession may be led from the midst of the congregation.

For those who experience oppression,
we pray, O God.

For those who are hungry and have no clothes,
we pray, O God.

For those who are experiencing homelessness,
we pray, O God.

When we refuse to break every yoke,
forgive us, O God.

When we persist in finger-pointing and wicked speech,
forgive us, O God.

When we participate in the oppression of others,
forgive us, O God.

As we prepare meals to feed the hungry,
give us a willing spirit, O God.

As we satisfy the needs of the afflicted,
give us a willing spirit, O God.

As we restore the streets where we live,
give us a willing spirit, O God.

Make our bones strong;
make us like a watered garden;
rebuild our ruins and give us peace. **Amen.**

INVITATION TO OFFERING

The invitation to offering may be led from the Communion table.

"For where your treasure is,
there your heart will be also."

With hearts full of gratitude,
let us give with gladness,
sharing the treasure of our faith with the world.

INVITATION TO THE TABLE

The invitation to the table is led from the Communion table.

> Remember the words of the prophet:
> the fast God chooses and the worship God desires
> is to share our bread with those who hunger.
>
> Let us gather at God's table,
> where Jesus feeds us with his body
> and sends us forth to feed others.

CHARGE

The blessing and charge may be led from the doors of the church.

> We enter this season with broken and contrite hearts,
> yet trusting that God loves us and will transform us.
> Return to God with your whole heart;
> our loving God is waiting with open arms.
> **Amen.** *or* **Thanks be to God.**

First Sunday in Lent

Genesis 9:8–17
Psalm 25:1–10

1 Peter 3:18–22
Mark 1:9–15

OPENING SENTENCES

> The time is fulfilled;
> the reign of God has come near.
> Repent, and believe the good news!
> **Lead us in your truth,**
> **O God of our salvation.**
>
> We come to worship the Beloved,
> the true child of God,
> with whom God is well pleased.
> **Help us to know your ways, O God,**
> **and teach us your paths.**

PRAYER OF THE DAY

> God of fulfilled promises,
> we gather today trusting
> in the signs you have shown us.
> Speak to us once again
> in this time together,
> as we seek to uphold our covenant with you. **Amen.**

INVITATION TO DISCIPLESHIP

The invitation to discipleship may be led from the baptismal font.

> In this season of Lent,
> we travel into our own wildernesses,
> confront our own mortality,
> and search for the coming of God.
>
> What is the wilderness in your soul?
> How are you longing for good news?
> What is the repentance you are being called to this season?

PRAYERS OF INTERCESSION

The prayers of intercession may be led from the midst of the congregation.

To you, O Lord, we lift our souls.
O God, in you we trust.

We enter the wilderness with fear and trembling:
afraid to face the sins we carry,
afraid to be measured and found wanting.
Remember us according to your steadfast love.
To you, O Lord, we lift our souls.
O God, in you we trust.

We enter the wilderness with tenderness and vulnerability:
lifting to you the uncertainty of our lives,
lifting to you our prayers for those we love.
Do not let us be put to shame.
To you, O Lord, we lift our souls.
O God, in you we trust.

We enter the wilderness with curiosity and hope:
longing for paths to be made clear,
longing for a deeper relationship with you.
Teach us your paths, O God of our salvation.
To you, O Lord, we lift our souls.
O God, in you we trust. Amen.

INVITATION TO OFFERING

The invitation to offering may be led from the Communion table.

We rejoice in the ways that God has saved us:
in the days of Noah and the flood,
through the life, death, and resurrection of Jesus Christ,
and through our own baptisms.

With gratitude for the gift of salvation,
we contribute to God's work in this world
through our offering.

INVITATION TO THE TABLE

The invitation to the table is led from the Communion table.

> This is the table of good news.
> This is the table prepared for us by Jesus,
> who suffered for us.
> This is the table set by Christ,
> who has gone to the right hand of God,
> with angels, authorities, and powers subject to him.
>
> This is the table where a cosmic God meets us,
> to share the bread and cup,
> to commune with us.

CHARGE

The blessing and charge may be led from the doors of the church.

> Let us go to seek signs of God's promise!
> Let us go to be people of God's covenant!
> **Amen.** *or* **Thanks be to God.**

Second Sunday in Lent

Genesis 17:1–7, 15–16
Psalm 22:23–31

Romans 4:13–25
Mark 8:31–38 *or*
Mark 9:2–9

OPENING SENTENCES

We stand as a witness to future generations:
God hears us when we cry out!

All the ends of the earth shall remember:
God does not turn from us!

We shall live for God,
and we will proclaim God's glory to all the earth!

PRAYER OF THE DAY

God of covenant, law, and faith,
we are here because of your faithfulness
throughout the generations.
You have kept your promises to our ancestors.
Guide us to be faithful to you,
that we too may share in the blessing
you offer us so freely. **Amen.**

---

*No distrust made [Abraham] waver concerning the
promise of God, but he grew strong in his faith as he
gave glory to God, being fully convinced that God
was able to do what [God] had promised. Therefore
his faith "was reckoned to him as righteousness."*

Romans 4:20–22

INVITATION TO DISCIPLESHIP

The invitation to discipleship may be led from the baptismal font.

During the season of Lent,
Christ's invitation to discipleship
is not always easy to hear:
"Those who want to save their life will lose it."
"If any want to become my followers,
let them deny themselves,
take up their cross, and follow me."

For today, let us sit in this discomfort.
Let us not brush away Jesus' words.
What is the cross you might be called to carry?
What do you cling to that is holding you back
from being who God calls you to be?

PRAYERS OF INTERCESSION

The prayers of intercession may be led from the midst of the congregation.

Almighty One,
as we come before you today,
we want to believe your promises,
but we find ourselves filled with doubt.

How can we not?
Despite our prayers,
despite our efforts,
there is still so much need in our world.

Like our ancestor in faith, Abraham,
we hope against hope.
We hope against hope that violence will cease.
We hope against hope that all might have their needs met.
We hope against hope that the earth will heal.
We hope against hope that justice will be upheld.

Even as we work for these hopes to come to reality,
we hold fast to your promises.
We believe in the vision
of peace, justice, and righteousness
that you proclaim to us in Scripture.
We believe that you are working alongside us,
giving us strength and renewing our spirits.
We believe that even when it seems impossible,
you are still with us.

Let our faith be reckoned to us as righteousness.
Let us see the fruits of this labor. **Amen.**

INVITATION TO OFFERING

The invitation to offering may be led from the Communion table.

As we continue in our Lenten journey,
we are called to set our minds not on human things
but on divine things.

As we offer our gifts today,
let us marvel at the transformation:
when we let go of these earthly offerings,
they are transformed to do the work of the divine.

INVITATION TO THE TABLE

The invitation to the table is led from the Communion table.

Our God does not despise us or ignore us
but spreads a feast before us.

The hungry and poor shall eat and be satisfied,
and those who seek God need look no further.
Here is God, with us at this table.

CHARGE

The blessing and charge may be led from the doors of the church.

Go forth in faith!
Amen. *or* **Thanks be to God.**

Third Sunday in Lent

Exodus 20:1–17   1 Corinthians 1:18–25
Psalm 19   John 2:13–22

OPENING SENTENCES

We come to be nourished by the Word of God.
We seek the wisdom of the Holy Spirit.

We come to be challenged by the commandments.
We seek the guidance of God, the Creator.

We come to be surprised by Jesus, our Savior.
We seek the foolishness of Christ, the crucified.

PRAYER OF THE DAY

Almighty One,
you have brought us here.
You have brought us through our trials
and have guided our path to this place
that we might join in praising you.
As we come to worship today,
help us remember your call on our lives,
that we might hold to your commandments always. **Amen.**

INVITATION TO DISCIPLESHIP

The invitation to discipleship may be led from the baptismal font.

Whether it is your first time or hundredth time
hearing these commandments of our God, listen:
"You shall have no other gods before me."
"You shall not make wrongful use of the name of the Lord."
"Remember the Sabbath day and keep it holy."

What do these words mean for your life here and now?
How can you commit to honoring these commandments this week?

PRAYERS OF INTERCESSION

The prayers of intercession may be led from the midst of the congregation.

O God, who has sculpted all creation,
your work is beautiful, vast, and glorious.
You have given us a world that flourishes,
commandments that teach us how to thrive,
and communities that encourage and support us.
We thank you for these gifts.

Yet we have failed in tending to these treasures.
We abuse the world for our own purposes,
we turn away from your guidance,
we wall ourselves away from others.
Cleanse us from our faults, hidden and revealed.

Our hearts ache, our world aches.
We offer these pains to you,
knowing that you are one who heals and restores.
We offer to you all who are in pain or ill health.
We offer to you all who do not have enough to get by.
We offer to you all who are grieving, anxious, or depressed.
We offer to you all who are trapped in feelings of shame.
We offer to you the world that is crying out for healing.
We offer to you the concerns
of our families, friends, and neighbors.

Let the words of our mouths
and the prayers of our hearts
be acceptable to you, O God,
our rock and redeemer. **Amen.**

INVITATION TO OFFERING

The invitation to offering may be led from the Communion table.

One of the only times we see Jesus truly angry
is when those in the temple
cared more about profit than prayer.
It is a sobering challenge for all of us;
we are called to use our resources to help this world,
instead of hoarding profit for ourselves.

In that spirit, let us offer our gifts to God.

INVITATION TO THE TABLE

The invitation to the table is led from the Communion table.

It may seem foolish—
this idea that sitting down and sharing a meal
can bring us into the presence of God
and form us into true community.
It may seem foolish—
this idea that the God who created the heavens and the earth,
who gives us commandments to follow
and wisdom to guide us,
would do something so commonplace as preparing a table
so all of us can eat together.

This is the beautiful foolishness of our faith.
Come to this table,
for God's foolishness is wiser than human wisdom,
and God's weakness is stronger than human strength.

CHARGE

The blessing and charge may be led from the doors of the church.

Let us go, proclaiming God's glory!
Let us go, filled with zeal for God's work!
Amen. *or* **Thanks be to God.**

Fourth Sunday in Lent

Numbers 21:4–9
Psalm 107:1–3, 17–22

Ephesians 2:1–10
John 3:14–21

OPENING SENTENCES

As we gather, we each bring with us
our own regrets, sins, and shames.
By grace we have been saved.

But we worship a God
who is rich in mercy!
By grace we have been saved.

We are what God has made us;
by grace we have been saved!
Let us worship our redeemer!

PRAYER OF THE DAY

Everlasting God,
you have gathered us in—
from east and west,
from north and south,
from all walks of life.
Pour out your Spirit on this time of worship,
that we might praise your deeds
with songs of joy! **Amen.**

*Let the redeemed of the LORD say so, those [God]
redeemed from trouble and gathered in from the lands,
from the east and from the west, from the north and
from the south.*

Psalm 107:2–3

INVITATION TO DISCIPLESHIP

The invitation to discipleship may be led from the baptismal font.

Even now, in the depth of Lent,
we remember that Christ came
not to condemn but to save.
No matter what we have done or failed to do,
Christ comes to us in love, offering salvation.

If you seek to live your life
in response to that great love,
join us here.
Join us in a continuous dance
of gratitude and praise.

PRAYERS OF INTERCESSION

The prayers of intercession may be led from the midst of the congregation.

God of salvation,
we have cried to you,
and you have delivered us.
We trust in your faithfulness
even when we cannot see the way forward.

We ask for your help and your presence—
in our own lives, our own struggles, our own hurts;
in the lives of those we hold dear;
in the lives of those who are struggling;
in the needs of this neighborhood;
in the soil and water of this earth;
in the global crises that seem so far beyond us.

We thank you for your love and guidance—
in the joys we celebrate,
in the possibilities we anticipate,
in the challenges we have overcome.

Send out your word to heal and deliver us.
Raise us up to you,
that we might know the immeasurable riches of your grace.
We give thanks to you, O God,
for your steadfast love endures forever. **Amen.**

INVITATION TO OFFERING

The invitation to offering may be led from the Communion table.

There is nothing we have done that has earned us salvation.
There is no price we pay for the grace of God.

As we bring forward these offerings,
we know this is not a payment, not a transaction,
but a gift we give out of gratitude
for all God has done for us.

INVITATION TO THE TABLE

The invitation to the table is led from the Communion table.

God does not leave us to die of hunger and thirst.
God does not leave us to be condemned.
God does not leave; God loves.
Here at this table we see signs,
manifestations of that love.
We see bread to nourish us and drink to sustain us.
We see a table set in love, grace, and mercy,
where we are raised and seated with Christ.

Come, for all has been made ready.

CHARGE

The blessing and charge may be led from the doors of the church.

Lift your eyes to Christ and believe!
We go, transformed by God's love.
Amen. *or* **Thanks be to God.**

Fifth Sunday in Lent

Jeremiah 31:31–34
Psalm 51:1–12 *or*
   Psalm 119:9–16

Hebrews 5:5–10
John 12:20–33

OPENING SENTENCES

> Create in me a clean heart, O God,
> and put a new and right spirit within me.
> **Do not cast me away from your presence,**
> **and do not take your Holy Spirit from me.**
>
> The Lord makes a new covenant with us
> and writes the law upon our hearts.
> **The Lord is our God,**
> **and we are God's people.**
>
> Let us seek the Lord
> **and treasure God's word in our hearts.**

PRAYER OF THE DAY

> Blessed are you, O Lord;
> you are ever faithful to your promises.
> Open our hearts to hear your voice
> in bellowing thunder and deafening silence,
> declaring the truths of salvation.
> Open our hearts to see your face
> in the sorrow of death and joy of life,
> making known the way of salvation.
> Open our hearts to glorify your name
> in faithful obedience and bold action,
> for you are the source of salvation. **Amen.**

INVITATION TO DISCIPLESHIP

The invitation to discipleship may be led from the baptismal font.

According to the abundant mercy of the Lord,
God has put the law of love within us
and has written it on our hearts
with the promise to be our God,
as we are God's people.

We who wish to see Jesus
have only to look upon our own hearts
in communion with the hearts of those around us,
for Jesus is seen and known here
in the community he is gathering to himself.

In these final days of Lent,
join us as we journey with Jesus to the cross,
that in dying to sin
we may be raised in steadfast love
and together bear abundant fruit.

PRAYERS OF INTERCESSION

The prayers of intercession may be led from the midst of the congregation.

God of covenantal love,
we wish to see Jesus,
who, in the days of his flesh,
offered up prayers and supplications
with passion and tearful agony.
Help us to see Christ at work in these days,
our great high priest who continues to pray
for the sake of this world.

Where we see hypocrisy and judgment
dividing your church,
we wish to see Jesus.

Help us to see Christ at work
in unlikely community,
in the bread and cup shared,
in imperfect expressions of love,
and in fruit born of discipleship.

Where we see pride and violence
tormenting the nations,
we wish to see Jesus.

Help us to see Christ at work
in the vulnerable and afraid
and in the poor and afflicted,
that we may see him glorified,
overturning structures of oppression.

Where we see destruction and greed
wreaking havoc on the earth,
we wish to see Jesus.

Help us to see Christ at work
in the ground that hides from our sight,
in the seed that will grow to bear fruit,
and in the body of our Lord
that will be raised to bring new life.

Where we see pain and sorrow
trying our loved ones,
we wish to see Jesus.

Help us to see Christ at work
in the suffering and dying,
and in troubled souls and cries of forsakenness,
that we may see him glorified,
healing all wounds and mending all brokenness.

Help us to see Christ at work, O Lord,
in these and all our prayers,
bearing the fruit of your glory.
For it is in Christ's name we pray. **Amen.**

INVITATION TO OFFERING

The invitation to offering may be led from the Communion table.

The psalmist declares:
I delight in the way of your decrees
as much as in all riches.

In grateful obedience, from the richness of our lives,
let us make an offering to God.

INVITATION TO THE TABLE

The invitation to the table is led from the Communion table.

Seeds have fallen into the earth,
dying that they may bear fruit—
bread to nourish the body
and wine to gladden the heart.
Christ was buried in the earth,
dying that we might live—
body broken to make us whole
and blood shed to bring forgiveness.

No matter how we have broken covenant with God,
Christ continues to spread the feast
of his faithfulness before us,
calling forth new life
and tending the fruit of his love.
If you wish to see Jesus,
come to the table of the Lord.

CHARGE

The blessing and charge may be led from the doors of the church.

Go forth in the abundant mercy of our God,
seek Jesus with your whole heart,
and bear the fruit of his kingdom.
For the one who gave himself over to death
has given this world new life.
Amen. *or* **Thanks be to God.**

Liturgy of the Palms/Passion

LITURGY OF THE PALMS
Psalm 118:1–2, 19–29
Mark 11:1–11 *or*
  John 12:12–16

LITURGY OF THE PASSION
Isaiah 50:4–9a
Psalm 31:9–16
Philippians 2:5–11
Mark 14:1–15:47 *or*
  Mark 15:1–39 (40–47)

The liturgy for Palm/Passion Sunday is designed for a day of stark contrast, a drama in two acts. It begins with a joyful procession into Jerusalem but ends with the somber journey to the cross. Worship planners are advised to resist the urge to avoid the theological tension inherent in the day by choosing between the palms and the passion. Rather, the fullness of Christian faith requires that we face the discomfort and live into the tension for the integrity of the gospel and for the sake of the world God loves.

The primary theological themes of Palm/Passion Sunday include the identity of the Suffering Servant and the ironic triumph and tragedy of Jesus' death, as shouts of celebration and a welcome fit for a king turn into cries of derision and a crown of thorns. Distinctive elements of the liturgy are the procession with palms and the poignant and extensive proclamation of Jesus' suffering and death; due to the nature and length of the Gospel reading, on Palm/Passion Sunday a brief sermon or time of contemplative silence may complete the proclamation of the word.

The resources that follow are intended to offer creativity, flexibility, and additional options for the church's celebration of Palm/Passion Sunday. Selected texts may be incorporated into the liturgies provided in denominational service books, such as the Presbyterian Church (U.S.A.) *Book of Common Worship* (pp. 263–71). Or they may be used in combination with other materials, found in this book or elsewhere, to develop new liturgies for Palm/Passion Sunday.

> *Then those who went ahead and those who followed were shouting, "Hosanna! Blessed is the one who comes in the name of the Lord!"*
>
> *Mark 11:9*

OPENING SENTENCES

Open to me the gates of righteousness,
that I may enter through them
and give thanks to the Lord.
This is the gate of the Lord;
the righteous shall enter through it.

The stone that the builders rejected
has become the chief cornerstone.
This is the Lord's doing;
it is marvelous in our eyes.

This is the day that the Lord has made;
let us rejoice and be glad in it.
Hosanna, we beseech you, O Lord!
Blessed is the one who comes in the name of the Lord.

PRAYER OF THE DAY

Holy One, we raise our palm branches
and lift our voices to cry "Hosanna!"
As we enter this Holy Week,
turn our hearts toward you,
that we may follow you past the parades
and into the shadows of betrayal, trial, and death.
As we enter this Holy Week,
let us worship you with our whole selves. **Amen.**

INVITATION TO DISCIPLESHIP

The invitation to discipleship may be led from the baptismal font.

Jesus enters Jerusalem
in a way that subverts the paradigm
of military parades, earthly might, and worldly honor.
He invites us to follow him in this way of peace.

If you are looking for an imperfect community
seeking to be faithful to Jesus,
there is room for you here.
Some days, like Peter, we falter.
But we have found that the journey is better together.
Join us.

PRAYERS OF INTERCESSION

The prayers of intercession may be led from the midst of the congregation.

O God, you are our God,
and we will offer you our praise
our whole lives long,
for your steadfast love endures forever.
Our lives are in your hands,
and we are grateful for your provision and care.

Our cries of "Hosanna!" will turn to "Crucify him!"
and our hearts break with that knowledge.
Mend our brokenness, and lead us to faithfulness.

Hear our prayers for the brokenness of this world.
We offer prayers this day for people who are hurt
by our greed, our judgment, our thirst for power.
Help us to mend what we have broken,
to repair relationships, to heal society.
Hosanna, **save us, Lord.**

We offer prayers for people in pain
and worry and grief.
Bring healing, bring comfort, bring wholeness.
Hosanna, **save us, Lord.**

Hear our prayers for the leaders of the world.
Whether they serve large or small communities,
cities, states, or countries,
may they follow your path of peace
rather than our warring ways.
Give them wisdom, humility,
and concern for your people,
that they may heal the world
rather than take from the spoils.
Hosanna, **save us, Lord.**

We offer these prayers in the name of the one
who came to serve rather than be served,
who was willing to take on the brokenness of the world
in order that it might be made whole.
Hosanna, **save us, Lord. Amen.**

INVITATION TO OFFERING

The invitation to offering may be led from the Communion table.

God's grace has been poured out on us,
in extravagant and inexplicable ways.

Let us respond in kind, in our offering,
that our gifts of time, talent, and treasure may combine,
overflowing with mercy and love for the world.

INVITATION TO THE TABLE

The invitation to the table is led from the Communion table.

The week Jesus was betrayed,
he was at the home of Simon,
and a woman poured out an extravagant gift
of perfume from an alabaster jar,
bathing his head with the ointment.
Many people at the table didn't understand the gift.
But when you recognize God's gift of grace
in the person of Jesus, as the woman did,
there is no response we could give that would be enough.

God's table is like that too.
Here we receive the bread and cup,
and our souls feast on the abundance of this meal.
We are prompted to live with extravagant and abundant grace,
sharing God's love freely with a hungry world.
Come, taste and see that the Lord is good.

CHARGE

The blessing and charge may be led from the doors of the church.

Go into this week with watchful hearts.
Be on the lookout for places
where this broken world needs our attention.
Be extravagant with expressions of love and care.
Be aware of how closely love and betrayal can exist together.
Offer chances for redemption.
Don't look away from the pain of the world; God is there.
Amen. *or* **Thanks be to God.**

The Three Days

The liturgy for the Three Days (or *Triduum*)—Holy Thursday, Good Friday, and the Great Vigil of Easter—is best understood as a single service in three parts. Together these events proclaim the mystery that is at the center of the church's calendar and the heart of Christian faith—the death and resurrection of Jesus Christ.

The primary theological themes of Holy Thursday include Christ's example of humble service and self-giving love. Distinctive elements of the liturgy are the act of foot washing and the celebration of the Eucharist or Lord's Supper, as well as the stripping of the church (removal of symbols and paraments) that may happen at its conclusion. The primary theological themes of Good Friday include God's compassion for the world, expressed through Jesus' passion on the cross, and the paradoxical nature of the atonement: strength from weakness, salvation from suffering, good from evil. Distinctive elements of the liturgy are the expansive prayers of intercession and Christ's lament in the solemn reproaches of the cross. The primary theological themes of the Great Vigil of Easter include God's saving work through history, culminating in Christ's resurrection, and the formation of church as covenant community and body of Christ. Distinctive elements of the liturgy are its four movements (Light, Readings, Baptism, and Eucharist) and its organization as a pilgrimage of the people of God.

The resources that follow are intended to offer creativity, flexibility, and additional options for the church's celebration of Holy Thursday, Good Friday, and the Great Vigil of Easter. Selected texts may be incorporated into the liturgies provided in denominational service books, such as the Presbyterian Church (U.S.A.) *Book of Common Worship* (pp. 272–304). Or they may be used in combination with other materials, found in this book or elsewhere, to develop new liturgies for the Three Days.

Holy Thursday

Exodus 12:1–4 (5–10), 11–14   1 Corinthians 11:23–26
Psalm 116:1–2, 12–19   John 13:1–17, 31b–35

OPENING SENTENCES

> A meal,
> a table,
> a group of friends.
> Water,
> bread,
> wine.
> **So simple,**
> **so powerful.**
>
> A promise: life abundant.
> A commandment: love one another.
> **Let the feast of love commence!**
> **Let us worship God!**

PRAYER OF THE DAY

> Gracious God, on this day
> when power is transformed into service
> and bread and wine turn into love,
> we ask that you teach us
> to humble ourselves,
> to share the abundance of this table,
> and to wash the feet of our enemies.
> Come and dwell in our hearts—
> feed us with your Word,
> and teach us how to love! **Amen.**

INVITATION TO DISCIPLESHIP

The invitation to discipleship may be led from a foot-washing basin or from the baptismal font.

Not by our hymns
or by the beauty of our buildings,
not by our theological claims
or by our fasting,
but by our love for one another—
by this, everyone will know we are Jesus' disciples.

You are invited
to join this community of love.

PRAYERS OF INTERCESSION

The prayers of intercession may be led from the midst of the congregation.

Holy God, on this day we remember
your mighty acts of deliverance—
as you freed those who were enslaved,
as you fed those who didn't know they were hungry,
as you washed the feet of those who would betray you.

Today we pray for our enemies—
for those who abuse their power
and perpetuate violence,
for those who do not love
all of your children.
In your mercy, **hear us, O God!**

Today we pray for those who hunger
for food and love,
for those who feel that hunger in their stomachs
and those who can feel it in their hearts.
In your mercy, **hear us, O God!**

Today we pray for those who are enslaved
by greedy companies,
by governments,
by the love of power and money.
In your mercy, **hear us, O God!**

You are the God who liberates,
the God who loves the world.
Teach us how to serve the world you love.
Teach us how to love the way you love. **Amen.**

INVITATION TO OFFERING

The invitation to offering may be led from the Communion table.

God has heard our voice and our supplications.
What shall we give in return
for all of God's bounty to us?

Let us offer our lives to the Lord.

INVITATION TO THE TABLE

The invitation to the table is led from the Communion table.

Love has prepared a feast for us—
for us to enjoy and be nourished
and receive Love's gifts,
even if we think we are not worthy.

Love is inviting us,
so come! The table is ready.

CHARGE

The blessing and charge may be led from the doors of the church.

Go out to this world and love one another—
with passion and humility,
through service,
through the sharing of a meal,
through forgiveness and compassion—
and holy Love will be with you,
now and forevermore.
Amen. *or* **Thanks be to God.**

The service continues on Good Friday.

Good Friday

Isaiah 52:13–53:12   Hebrews 10:16–25 *or*
Psalm 22   Hebrews 4:14–16; 5:7–9
                                        John 18:1–19:42

OPENING SENTENCES

> The psalmist prayed,
> "On you I was cast from birth."
> **And Jesus said,**
> **"Here is your son."**
>
> The psalmist prayed,
> "I am poured out like water."
> **And Jesus said,**
> **"I am thirsty."**
>
> The psalmist prayed,
> "God has accomplished it!"
> **And Jesus said,**
> **"It is finished."**

PRAYER OF THE DAY

> Holy God,
> we come to bear witness
> to the suffering and death
> of the one you sent to save us.
> Hold us in your presence
> as we approach the cross.
> Fill us with your passion
> as we proclaim the gospel.
> Use us as your people
> as we pray for the world.
> Bless us with your peace
> as we depart in silence.
> Keep us in your promise
> as we await the dawn.
> In Jesus' name we pray. **Amen.**

INVITATION TO DISCIPLESHIP

The invitation to discipleship may be led from the baptismal font.

In Jesus Christ we have a great high priest
who has passed through the heavens—
one who can sympathize with our weakness
because he has been tested as we are,
yet without sin.

You are invited to come to Christ—
to lay down your burdens and sorrows,
your guilt, your doubt, and your fear;
to take up his cross and follow him
as he leads us from death to life.

PRAYERS OF INTERCESSION

The prayers of intercession may be led from the midst of the congregation.

Other intercessions may be added; ample times of silence should be provided.

Holy One, we remember how,
in the days of his flesh,
Jesus offered up prayers and supplications
with loud cries and tears
to the one who was able to save him from death.

Hear us as we join his prayer.

For those who are wounded and disfigured . . .

For those whose appearance is not desirable . . .

For those despised and avoided by us . . .

For those we don't even think about . . .

For those who suffer and know sickness well . . .

For those who bear our sickness and suffering . . .

For those who are afflicted and tormented . . .

For those who are pierced because of our rebellion . . .

For those who are crushed because of our crimes . . .

For those who wonder why you have forsaken them . . .

In all things, O God,
we approach the throne of grace with boldness.
Show us your mercy.
Give us your grace.
Help us
and all for whom we pray
in this hour of need;
through Jesus Christ our Lord. **Amen.**

SOLEMN REPROACHES OF THE CROSS

O my beloveds, my church,
what have I done to you,
or in what have I offended you?

I formed you from stardust and love
and gave you a home full of birds and trees
and taught you how to love,
but you have prepared a cross for your Savior.
Lord, have mercy.

I heard your cries
and liberated you from slavery.
I led you to a land flowing with milk and honey,
but you have prepared a cross for your Savior.
Lord, have mercy.

I walked with you through the wilderness
and sheltered you from the scorching sun.
I provided food and water as you wandered,
but you have prepared a cross for your Savior.
Lord, have mercy.

I brought you back from exile
and restored your homeland.
I rebuilt your cities and your nation,
but you have prepared a cross for your Savior.
Lord, have mercy.

I came to dwell among you
and showed you a new way of being.
I poured out my love for you,
but you have prepared a cross for your Savior.
Lord, have mercy.

I sent my Holy Spirit
and promised to never leave you.
I set your hearts on fire,
but you have prepared a cross for your Savior.
Lord, have mercy.

*The service continues at the Great Vigil of Easter or on the Resurrection of
the Lord.*

Great Vigil of Easter

Twelve readings from the Hebrew Scriptures are provided for the Service of Readings in the Great Vigil of Easter. At least three should be chosen; the Exodus reading is always included. Psalms or canticles are provided as a musical response to each reading.

1. Genesis 1:1–2:4a
   Psalm 136:1–9, 23–26
2. Genesis 7:1–5, 11–18; 8:6–18; 9:8–13
   Psalm 46
3. Genesis 22:1–18
   Psalm 16
4. Exodus 14:10–31; 15:20–21
   Exodus 15:1b–13, 17–18
5. Baruch 3:9–15; 3:32–4:4 *or* Proverbs 8:1–8, 19–21; 9:4b–6
   Psalm 19
6. Isaiah 55:1–11
   Isaiah 12:2–6
7. Isaiah 61:1–4, 9–11
   Deuteronomy 32:1–4, 7, 36a, 43a
8. Ezekiel 36:24–28
   Psalms 42 and 43
9. Ezekiel 37:1–14
   Psalm 143
10. Daniel 3:1–29
    Song of the Three Young Men 35–65
11. Jonah 1:1–2:1
    Jonah 2:2–3 (4–6), 7–9
12. Zephaniah 3:14–20
    Psalm 98

The Service of Readings continues with the Epistle (and its Psalm response) and Gospel:

Romans 6:3–11
Psalm 114
John 20:1–18

OPENING SENTENCES

This is the night
when we gather at the fire of new creation.
Jesus Christ is the light of the world.

This is the night
when we tell the story of salvation.
Jesus Christ is the Word made flesh.

This is the night
when we cross the sea of liberation.
Jesus Christ is living water.

This is the night
when we share the feast of redemption.
Jesus Christ is the bread of life.

PRAYER OF THE DAY

God of all glory, we rejoice this night
at the splendor of your saving work.
Through Christ you have redeemed us
from our bondage to sin and death.
We give you thanks this night
that you have never forsaken us—
in the passage through the sea,
in the wilderness of wandering,
and in the harrowing of hell.
By the fire of your Holy Spirit,
let your righteousness be revealed,
let your justice overcome evil,
and let your peace forever reign,
on earth as it is in heaven;
through Christ, the Morning Star. **Amen.**

INVITATION TO DISCIPLESHIP

The invitation to discipleship may be led from the baptismal font.

Water has carried us to this place.

We felt the Spirit of God
moving over deep waters
on the eve of creation.

We saw the waters of the flood
wash away the sin of the earth
in the days of Noah.

We heard the people of God
singing songs of freedom
by the waters of the sea.

We tasted the water of life
when the prophet called us:
Come, all who thirst.

Now we come to the water of baptism,
where we share the dying and rising
of Jesus Christ our Lord.

Will you turn to the living God
and turn away from evil? **I will.**

Will you trust in Jesus Christ
as your Savior and Lord? **I will.**

Will you be guided by the Spirit
as you live out your faith? **I will.**

A prayer of thanksgiving over the water or thanksgiving for baptism follows.

INVITATION TO THE TABLE

The invitation to the table is led from the Communion table.

Let everyone who thirsts come to the waters!
Let everyone who hungers come to the feast!
As the rain comes down from heaven to water the earth,
the Spirit of God will be poured out on all flesh.
As the seed comes up from the earth to become bread,
the Word of God will raise us from death to life.

This is the table of the Lord.
Come, taste and see the grace of God.

CHARGE

The blessing and charge may be led from the doors of the church.

With the warmth of the fire
and the words of the story,
in the power of the water
and the fullness of the meal,
go and tell this good news to all:
Christ is risen!
Christ is risen!
Christ is risen indeed!
Alleluia! Amen.

SEASON OF EASTER

Making Connections

The "great fifty days" of Easter provide an extended season for the church's celebration of the resurrection of Jesus from the dead. As Sunday stands in relation to the week, the seven weeks of Easter stand in relation to the year. Indeed, the season of Easter is approximately one-seventh of the length of the year, just as Sunday is one-seventh of a week. If Sunday is known among Christians as "the Lord's Day," then Easter might be called "the Lord's Season."

At first glance, this extended time of celebration seems incongruent with the abrupt ending of Mark's Gospel. Matthew, Luke, and John all devote their closing words to the resurrection appearances of Jesus: in Matthew, the Great Commission (Matt. 28:16–20); in Luke, the road to Emmaus (Luke 24:13–35), a meal of broiled fish (Luke 24:36–43), the interpretation of the Scriptures (Luke 24:44–49), and the ascension (Luke 24:50–52); in John, the gift of the Spirit (John 20:19–23), the meeting with Thomas (John 20:24–29), a breakfast on the beach (John 21:1–14), and conversations with Peter (John 21:15–25). Mark, by contrast, ends with three women fleeing from an empty tomb in silence, wonder, and fear (Mark 16:1–8). Alternate endings of Mark's Gospel ("intermediate" and "longer") seek to flesh out the resurrection with accounts of Jesus' appearances to the disciples, commissioning, and ascension into heaven, but these seem to have been appended by later editors, a kind of apology for Mark's hasty "exit stage left."

But maybe this is the genius of Mark's Gospel. Mark turns "immediately" to the "so what" of the empty tomb—setting the stage for our response and inviting us to tell our own resurrection stories. How will *we* proclaim this good news? How will we live in the light of Easter morning? How will we look for the risen Lord among us?

As you celebrate the season of Easter, be on the lookout for contemporary signs of new life in Jesus Christ. Preach and pray with the confidence that the Lord *is* risen, present and active in our world. Bear witness to the life-giving power of the gospel in your community of faith. Show and tell the good news that Christ is risen indeed through acts of service and love.

The real ending to Mark's Gospel is in God's hands—being written here and now in the mission of the church and the life of the world. This is the day of the Lord. This is the season of resurrection.

Seasonal/Repeating Resources

These resources are intended for regular use throughout the season of Easter.

CONFESSION AND PARDON

The confession and pardon may be led from the baptismal font.

> Jesus Christ is the love of God made flesh,
> the love that even death could not destroy.
> There is no fear in love,
> for fear has to do with punishment;
> but perfect love casts out fear.

> Trusting in God's grace, let us confess our sin.

The confession may begin with a time of silence for personal prayer.

> **Living God, your Son, Jesus Christ,**
> **taught us how to love you,**
> **one another, and ourselves.**
> **We confess that we have failed**
> **to embody such love.**
> **We turn away from you,**
> **failing to love and serve you**
> **with heart and mind**
> **and soul and strength.**
> **We turn away from others**
> **who are poor and oppressed,**
> **are different from us,**
> **or do not share our views.**
> **We turn away from ourselves,**
> **even though you made us in your image**
> **and have claimed us in Christ**
> **as your own beloved children.**

Merciful God, forgive us
for not loving you, others, and ourselves.
Soften our hearts of stone,
and transform us into living signs
of your love in the world;
in the name of the risen Lord.

Water may be poured or lifted from the baptismal font.

God is love,
and those who abide in love
abide in God,
and God abides in them.
We love because God first loved us.

In the name of Jesus Christ, we are forgiven.
Thanks be to God.

PRAYER FOR ILLUMINATION

The prayer for illumination is led from the lectern or pulpit.

Holy God,
as we gather this day
in the presence of the risen Lord,
send your Holy Spirit
to open our minds and hearts,
that we may understand your words
and live them out in the world
as a sign of new life for all;
through Jesus Christ our Savior. **Amen.**

THANKSGIVING FOR BAPTISM

The thanksgiving for baptism is led from the baptismal font.

The introductory dialogue ("The Lord be with you . . .") may be sung or spoken.

Gracious God, we thank you
that in every age you have made water
a sign of your presence.

In the beginning
your Spirit brooded over the waters,
and they became the source of all creation.

You led your people Israel
through the waters of the Red Sea
to their new land of freedom and hope.

In the waters of the Jordan
your Son was baptized by John
and anointed with your Spirit for his ministry.

May this same Spirit bless this water today.
May this be the water
through which we experience your healing and wholeness,
through which we hear your voice speaking in our hearts.

Come, Holy Spirit, come.
Renew us and make us whole.

Come, Holy Spirit, come.
Speak into the hearts of all gathered today.

Come, Holy Spirit, come.
Fill us with desire for your justice and peace,
your liberation and life,
now and every day. **Amen.**

GREAT THANKSGIVING

The Great Thanksgiving is led from the Communion table.

The introductory dialogue ("The Lord be with you . . .") may be sung or spoken.

> All glory, all honor, all praise to you, O God.
> The floods clap their hands, the hills sing with joy,
> and the whole earth declares your saving work.
> You call us to be planted like trees by the water,
> meditating on your word night and day
> and bearing good fruit in due season.
> Even when we pass through deep valleys,
> you walk beside us and comfort us.
> You prepare a table for us in times of trouble;
> with grace, you fill our cups to overflowing.
>
> With psalms, hymns, and spiritual songs,
> we offer our thanks and praise:

The Sanctus ("Holy, holy, holy . . .") may be sung or spoken.

> We praise you for Jesus Christ our Lord.
> He came to be our good shepherd—
> offering green pastures and still waters
> and leading us in paths of righteousness.
> When he was given over to the cross,
> he rose from the dead to everlasting life,
> that we might share the gift of salvation.

The words of institution are included here, if not elsewhere, while the bread and cup are lifted (but not broken/poured).

> You have put gladness in our hearts, O God,
> more than when grain and wine abound.
> Therefore we offer our hearts and lives to you
> as we share this feast of grace.

A memorial acclamation ("Christ has died . . .") may be sung or spoken.

Send forth your Holy Spirit, O God,
to renew the face of the earth.
Open your hand to fill us with good things,
and give us our food in due season—
the body and blood of Christ,
bread of life and cup of salvation.

Teach us to live together in unity,
and give us the blessing of life forevermore.
Lead us across the River Jordan
and into the freedom of your promised land.

Then we will praise you, O Lord,
joining the song of the great congregation,
the nations of the world,
those who sleep in the earth,
and all people yet unborn.

Until that day, we bless you, O God,
singing your praise with all our hearts.

A Trinitarian doxology and Great Amen may be sung or spoken.

PRAYER AFTER COMMUNION

The prayer after Communion is led from the Communion table.

Living God, provider of all things,
we thank you for this bread and cup,
signs of the presence of the risen Lord.
Strengthen us through your Holy Spirit,
that we may live in unity as Christ's body
and proclaim your love to all the world.
In the name of Jesus Christ we pray. **Amen.**

PRAYER OF THANKSGIVING

The prayer of thanksgiving may be led from the Communion table.

Merciful God, with humble hearts
we give you thanks for all your grace—
for the wondrous work of your creation,
the blessing of your providence,
and the saving mystery of faith.
By the power of your Holy Spirit,
reveal your living presence among us.
Help us to share our gifts with others,
to serve your mission in the world,
and to tell the good news of resurrection;
through Jesus Christ our Lord. **Amen.**

BLESSING

The blessing and charge may be led from the doors of the church.

May the Lord our God bless you,
may Christ the shepherd lead you,
and may the Holy Spirit sustain you
this day and forevermore. **Alleluia!**

Easter Day/Resurrection of the Lord

Acts 10:34–43 *or*
  Isaiah 25:6–9
Psalm 118:1–2, 14–24

1 Corinthians 15:1–11 *or*
  Acts 10:34–43
Mark 16:1–8 *or* John 20:1–18

OPENING SENTENCES

> This is the day the Lord has made;
> **let us rejoice and be glad in it!**

> Testify to what we have seen:
> Jesus Christ is risen!
> **Alleluia! He is risen indeed!**

PRAYER OF THE DAY

> Infinite God,
> your light breaks forth like the dawn,
> scattering the darkness
> and renewing our hope.
> You are our joy and our life,
> the wellspring of our praise,
> the font of all our alleluias.
> All glory and honor to you, O God,
> through Jesus Christ our Lord. **Amen.**

INVITATION TO DISCIPLESHIP

The invitation to discipleship may be led from the baptismal font.

> This is the day that life overcame death.
> This is the day that love vanquished hate.

> Our risen Lord waits with open arms
> to welcome you to new life in him,
> from this day forth.

PRAYERS OF INTERCESSION

The prayers of intercession may be led from the midst of the congregation.

Allow for periods of spoken or silent prayer.

The Lord for whom we have waited has come;
he is risen and in our midst.
Let us then bring our intercessions, saying,
Lord, hear our prayer:
Your steadfast love endures forever.

For your church around the world,
around this country,
in this community,
and this congregation . . .
Make us ever more faithful,
our eyes always on Jesus.
Lord, hear our prayer:
Your steadfast love endures forever.

For your world and its rulers,
our government and our local leaders . . .
Give them your wisdom,
establish your justice,
and imbue us with peace.
Lord, hear our prayer:
Your steadfast love endures forever.

For this earth that lives and breathes with us,
the waters that flow and all that grows,
for every living creature . . .

Local waters and lands may be named.

Enable us to flourish,
and teach us to live as one.
Lord, hear our prayer:
Your steadfast love endures forever.

For those who are ill,
those facing death,
and those who care for them . . .
Grant your healing mercies
and bestow your peace.
Lord, hear our prayer:
Your steadfast love endures forever.

For those without hope,
those who mourn,
those who seek to know you . . .
Bathe us in light,
and fill us with your grace.
Lord, hear our prayer:
Your steadfast love endures forever.

All this we pray through our Savior and friend,
Jesus Christ. **Amen.**

INVITATION TO OFFERING

The invitation to offering may be led from the Communion table.

The stone has been rolled away,
and Christ is loose in the world.

Bring your best gifts today,
and join in the work he is doing.

INVITATION TO THE TABLE

The invitation to the table is led from the Communion table.

Christ is risen, and the feast is ready!
He has laid the table and invites all who love him
to share the meal he has prepared.

Come and join the feast.

CHARGE

The blessing and charge may be led from the doors of the church.

Go and tell the good news of Jesus Christ:
He is risen!
He is life.
He is love.
Amen. *or* **Thanks be to God.**

Easter Evening/ Resurrection of the Lord

Isaiah 25:6–9   1 Corinthians 5:6b–8
Psalm 114   Luke 24:13–49

OPENING SENTENCES

Christ our Lord is risen from the dead.
Alleluia!

Proclaim the good news for all to hear:
Jesus Christ is the lord of life;
he has swallowed up death forever.

PRAYER OF THE DAY

God of grace,
who raised Christ Jesus to new life,
we praise you.
God of power,
whose Spirit gathers us today,
we thank you.
God of glory,
who gives us new life,
we bless you.
This is the day you, the Lord, have made,
and we rejoice in you,
through Jesus Christ. **Amen.**

INVITATION TO DISCIPLESHIP

The invitation to discipleship may be led from the baptismal font.

Are you seeking new life? Come.
Have you lost hope? Oh, come.

Are you looking for the light?
Then come to Jesus,
who waits with open arms.

PRAYERS OF INTERCESSION

The prayers of intercession may be led from the midst of the congregation.

God promises to hear every prayer,
to wipe away every tear.
Let us bring our burdens to God, saying,
God of life, **hear our prayer.**

Sovereign God,
lead us in the ways of peace.
Establish justice in every land.
Grant wisdom to all those who lead.
God of life, **hear our prayer.**

Saving God, bless your church.
Where there is apathy, bring new life.
Where there is growth, keep love the aim.
Where there is oppression or persecution,
protect and comfort.
God of life, **hear our prayer.**

God of peace, bring an end to violence
in our world,
in our communities,
in our homes.
Show us a better way.
God of life, **hear our prayer.**

Creating God, you made the world and called it good.
Cleanse our waterways and ensure water for all.
Clear the air and the earth of poison,
and teach us to live in harmony with all you have made.
God of life, **hear our prayer.**

Healing God, pour out your mercies on those who suffer:
those with diseases and the chronically ill,
those in mental or emotional anguish,
those who live with addiction.
God of life, **hear our prayer.**

Resurrecting God, be with those who are dying,
those who care for them,
and those who love them.
Grant them the peace that passes all understanding,
and receive those who die into your merciful arms.
God of life, **hear our prayer.**

Eternal God, keep us faithful until the day
when Christ returns to make all things new.
Then may we join you and the whole host of heaven
to sing your praises forevermore.
Through Christ
and by the power of the Holy Spirit
we pray. **Amen.**

INVITATION TO OFFERING

The invitation to offering may be led from the Communion table.

God has defeated every evil
and vanquished death forever.

Bring your gifts of thanksgiving;
bring your offerings with joy,
that all may know the good news of the gospel.

INVITATION TO THE TABLE

The invitation to the table is led from the Communion table.

After a long day, walking the road to Emmaus,
Jesus sat at table with his two companions.
He took bread, blessed it, and broke it,
and their eyes were opened and they recognized him.

Christ invites us to this table,
that he might feed us with the bread of life
and we might know him more.

CHARGE

The blessing and charge may be led from the doors of the church.

Go and tell what you have seen and heard:
Jesus Christ is risen today!
Amen. *or* **Thanks be to God.**

Second Sunday of Easter

Acts 4:32–35   1 John 1:1–2:2
Psalm 133   John 20:19–31

OPENING SENTENCES

How good and pleasant it is
when kindred live together in unity!
**Let us gather together in the light,
giving praise to our God.**

PRAYER OF THE DAY

God of life,
you raised Christ from the dead,
that we might share in his life.
He breathes into us your Holy Spirit
and forgives all our sins.
Gather us in today, that we might sing your praise
and hear your good news,
giving thanks with our very lives. **Amen.**

INVITATION TO DISCIPLESHIP

The invitation to discipleship may be led from the baptismal font.

Come, all you who are seeking peace,
for Jesus Christ promises to bless us.

Whether you are meeting Christ for the first time,
or renewing your faith in him,
Jesus waits to welcome you.

PRAYERS OF INTERCESSION

The prayers of intercession may be led from the midst of the congregation.

God of life, hear us as we pray.
In sound and silence,
we pour out our hearts to you,
depending on the Spirit to intercede for us
with sighs too deep for words.

For your church in every place . . .
Holy Spirit, **pray with us.**

For peace in every land and every home . . .
Holy Spirit, **pray with us.**

For the power to forgive
and the humility to ask forgiveness . . .
Holy Spirit, **pray with us.**

For healing for those who suffer . . .
Holy Spirit, **pray with us.**

For justice where there is oppression
and understanding where there is division . . .
Holy Spirit, **pray with us.**

For those without homes or food,
love or safety . . .
Holy Spirit, **pray with us.**

For those needs closest to our hearts
and those known only to you . . .
Holy Spirit, **pray with us.**

God of heaven and earth,
receive our prayers,
however ragged they may be,
and accomplish your work in the world.
Keep us faithful and hopeful
until Christ comes to make all things well.
In his name we pray. **Amen.**

INVITATION TO OFFERING

The invitation to offering may be led from the Communion table.

Christ invites us to bring our gifts to his table,
sharing what we have with any in need,
proclaiming the good news of love
in all we say and do.

With generous hearts,
let us bring our offerings to God.

INVITATION TO THE TABLE

The invitation to the table is led from the Communion table.

This is the table of our risen Lord, Jesus Christ.
Come if your faith is strong,
or if you are full of fear and doubt.
Come in joy or in sorrow,
hope or despair.

Whatever you carry,
this meal is for you,
and Jesus himself invites you.

CHARGE

The blessing and charge may be led from the doors of the church.

Go in peace,
walking in the light of Christ.
Amen. *or* **Thanks be to God.**

Third Sunday of Easter

Acts 3:12–19

1 John 3:1–7

Psalm 4

Luke 24:36b–48

OPENING SENTENCES

Children of God, rejoice!
Alleluia!

For the one who was promised,
the Messiah of God,
has been raised in new life for us.
Children of God, rejoice!
Alleluia!

PRAYER OF THE DAY

Everlasting God,
in Jesus Christ you embodied the words of the prophets.
In Jesus Christ you renew our hope for the future.
For he is risen, and he is Lord.
Make us witnesses to this good news,
and keep us strong
until he comes again in glory.
In Jesus' name we pray. **Amen.**

INVITATION TO DISCIPLESHIP

The invitation to discipleship may be led from the baptismal font.

Christ stands before us,
bestowing his grace,
teaching us his truth,
and showing us the way.

If you would follow him—
for the first time or for the hundredth time—
come, for he waits to embrace you.

PRAYERS OF INTERCESSION

The prayers of intercession may be led from the midst of the congregation.

Let us bring our intercessions to the Lord, saying,
Be gracious, O God;
hear our prayer.

The world is a dangerous place, O God.
Quell violence.
Foster peace.
Cultivate understanding where this is none.
Be gracious, O God;
hear our prayer.

The world is a beautiful place, O God.
Your creation is full of glory;
your works fill us with awe.
Make us better caretakers of the planet,
and teach us to live in concert with all you have made.
Be gracious, O God;
hear our prayer.

The world is a wounded place, O God.
Heal the hurts and illnesses of the body.
Soothe troubles of the mind and sorrows of the heart.
Mend divisions between parties and peoples.
Be gracious, O God;
hear our prayer.

The world is a blessed place, O God.
Teach us to be agents of blessing;
to build up and not tear down,
to lift up all that is good,
to foster kindness and notice grace.
Be gracious, O God;
hear our prayer.

The world is a scary place, O God.
Bolster our courage to stand for justice.
Replace our fear with faith in your work.
Keep before us the vision of the world
that is to come,
your reign of justice and peace,
a realm where love prevails.

And make us ready for the day when Christ will come
and make this world whole.
In his name we pray. **Amen.**

INVITATION TO OFFERING

The invitation to offering may be led from the Communion table.

Whatever you have to give,
give it cheerfully,
knowing that God can do
anything we can ask or imagine.

Bring your offerings to God
with glad and generous hearts.

INVITATION TO THE TABLE

The invitation to the table is led from the Communion table.

When Jesus met his disciples after he was raised,
he asked them for something to eat.
Here at this table
he has laid a feast,
that we might enjoy communion with him
and with one another.

So come to the table;
there is room for us all.

CHARGE

The blessing and charge may be led from the doors of the church.

Go and tell what you have seen:
Christ is alive
and at work in this world,
guiding our steps along the way.
Amen. *or* **Thanks be to God.**

Fourth Sunday of Easter

Acts 4:5–12   1 John 3:16–24
Psalm 23   John 10:11–18

OPENING SENTENCES

> Jesus says:
> I am the good shepherd.
> **The good shepherd**
> **lays down his life for the sheep.**
>
> Jesus says:
> I know my own,
> and my own know me.
> **Jesus is the good shepherd.**
> **Let us worship God.**

PRAYER OF THE DAY

> Holy One, we give you thanks
> that you sent Jesus to guide us
> in your way of truth and life.
> Help us to listen to his voice
> and follow him faithfully.
> Teach us to show welcome
> to the other members of the flock
> you draw into your fold.
> Show us how to devote our lives
> to the service of the gospel;
> in Jesus' name we pray. **Amen.**

INVITATION TO DISCIPLESHIP

The invitation to discipleship may be led from the baptismal font.

Jesus Christ was crucified,
but God raised him from the dead
as a sign of new life and hope for all.
The stone that the builders rejected
has become the cornerstone;
all are welcome in God's house.

Come with us and follow Christ,
the crucified and risen Lord.
There is a place for you in God's house.

PRAYERS OF INTERCESSION

The prayers of intercession may be led from the midst of the congregation.

Lord, you are our shepherd
and the guardian of all who are in need.
Hear our prayer.

We pray for those who are troubled . . .
Let them lie down in green pastures,
and lead them beside still waters.

We pray for those who have lost their way . . .
Restore their souls,
and lead them in right paths,
for your name's sake.

We pray for those who are in danger . . .
Walk with them through deep valleys,
and let them fear no evil;
comfort them with your rod and staff.

We pray for those who are oppressed . . .
Prepare a table for them
in the presence of their enemies;
anoint them with your Spirit,
that their cups may overflow.
God of all goodness and mercy,
be with us all the days of our lives,
and let us dwell in your house forever;
through Jesus Christ our Lord. **Amen.**

INVITATION TO OFFERING

The invitation to offering may be led from the Communion table.

This is what we know about God's love:
Jesus laid down his life for us,
and we are called to lay down our lives for one another.
How does God's love abide in anyone
who has the world's goods and,
seeing another person in need, refuses to help?

Let us love as Jesus loves.
Let us put our faith into action.
Let us offer our lives to the Lord.

INVITATION TO THE TABLE

The invitation to the table is led from the Communion table.

As a good shepherd feeds the flock,
the Lord has prepared a table for us.

Come to the table of the Lord,
and share in this holy feast of love.

CHARGE

The blessing and charge may be led from the doors of the church.

Children of God,
let us love one another,
not only in word or speech
but in truth and action.
This is Christ's commandment.
Amen. *or* **Thanks be to God.**

Fifth Sunday of Easter

Acts 8:26–40   1 John 4:7–21
Psalm 22:25–31   John 15:1–8

OPENING SENTENCES

Beloved, let us love one another,
because love is from God;
everyone who loves is born of God
and knows God.

God's love was revealed among us in this way:
God sent the beloved Son into the world
that we might live through him.
Beloved, since God loved us so much,
we also ought to love one another.

God is love,
and those who abide in love abide in God,
and God abides in them.
We love because God first loved us.

PRAYER OF THE DAY

O Lord God, we give you thanks
that through Jesus Christ
you have made us branches of your vine.
Help us to abide in Christ
and be disciples of your Word,
that we may live and grow in him
and bear good fruit for the world;
through Jesus Christ our Lord. **Amen.**

INVITATION TO DISCIPLESHIP

The invitation to discipleship may be led from the baptismal font.

> We give thanks to God for the gift of baptism.
> As the Ethiopian eunuch believed in God
> and was baptized by Philip,
> we trust that God chooses and claims us,
> empowering us with the Holy Spirit.
>
> You are invited to share this life with us,
> living into the promises of our baptism
> and following God's way in the world.

PRAYERS OF INTERCESSION

The prayers of intercession may be led from the midst of the congregation.

> Jesus said: If you abide in me
> and my words abide in you,
> ask for whatever you wish
> and it will be done for you.
> In this spirit and with this confidence
> we make our prayers to the Lord.
>
> We pray for people who are poor . . .
> By your grace, O God,
> set before them an abundant feast.
>
> We pray for those who are afraid . . .
> Empower them with your perfect love,
> the love that casts out all fear.
>
> We pray for new believers . . .
> Welcome them into the body of Christ,
> and fill them with your Holy Spirit.
>
> We pray for those who feel cut off . . .
> Abide with them, O God,
> as branches of your vine.
>
> O Lord our God, fulfill your word in us,
> that we may join with all the earth
> and with generations past, present, and future
> in proclaiming your wondrous work;
> through Jesus Christ our Savior. **Amen.**

INVITATION TO OFFERING

The invitation to offering may be led from the Communion table.

> We are branches of the vine.
> Apart from God, we can do nothing.
> But if we abide in Christ,
> Christ will abide in us,
> and we will bear good fruit.
>
> Let us gather up the offering of our lives.
> Let us present our gifts to the Lord.

INVITATION TO THE TABLE

The invitation to the table is led from the Communion table.

> At this table, the poor will eat and be satisfied;
> all who seek God will praise the Lord.
>
> Let us lift up our hearts with praise and thanksgiving
> as we share this joyful feast.

CHARGE

The blessing and charge may be led from the doors of the church.

> Remember the words of Jesus:
> I am the vine; you are the branches.
> Abide in me as I abide in you,
> and you will bear much good fruit.
> **Amen.** *or* **Thanks be to God.**

Sixth Sunday of Easter

Acts 10:44–48   1 John 5:1–6
Psalm 98   John 15:9–17

OPENING SENTENCES

>Sing to the Lord a new song,
>for God has done marvelous things!
>**Sing of God's great faithfulness**
>**and steadfast love to all.**
>
>Make a joyful noise to the Lord, all the earth;
>sing praises!
>**Rejoice in the presence of God,**
>**who reigns with equity and justice.**

PRAYER OF THE DAY

>Loving God, you sent your only Son
>to lay down his life for the world.
>Teach us to love one another
>as Christ has first loved us.
>Draw us closer to Christ in love,
>not as servants but as friends.
>Help us to keep his commandments,
>that our joy may be complete,
>abiding in your love forever;
>through Jesus Christ our Lord. **Amen.**

---

*"This is my commandment, that you love one another as
I have loved you. No one has greater love than this, to lay
down one's life for one's friends."*

John 15:12–13

INVITATION TO DISCIPLESHIP

The invitation to discipleship may be led from the baptismal font.

The Lord God has promised
to pour out the Holy Spirit on all flesh.
Peter witnessed this wonder
when the Holy Spirit descended
upon all who heard the word of God,
Gentiles and Jews alike.
As the wind blows where it chooses,
the grace of God overflows for all.

Are you ready to draw closer to Christ
through the sacrament of baptism?
Or are you longing to be more faithful
in living out your baptismal promises?
We are here for you, ready to accompany you
on the journey of discipleship.

PRAYERS OF INTERCESSION

The prayers of intercession may be led from the midst of the congregation.

Holy God, you call us to live in love
and to be a sign of your great love for the world.
Hear our prayers.

Give us love for your church . . .
Keep us faithful in proclaiming the word,
celebrating the sacraments,
and serving all who are in need.

Give us love for the earth . . .
Teach us to care for and protect
the good world you have created
and all the creatures who share our home.

Give us love for all people . . .
Lead us to work for justice and peace,
liberating those who are oppressed
and putting an end to violence.

Give us love for our neighbors . . .
Fill us with compassion and concern
for the people in our communities
who are vulnerable or in distress.

Give us love for one another . . .
Use us as instruments of healing,
tending to the sick and suffering
and comforting those who mourn.

Give us love for your holy realm . . .
Make us ready and eager for the day
when Christ will come again
in the glory of your new creation.

Abide in us, loving God,
and help us to abide in you;
through Jesus Christ our Lord. **Amen.**

INVITATION TO OFFERING

The invitation to offering may be led from the Communion table.

The commandments of God are not burdensome.
We are called to love the Lord our God
and to love one another as Christ loves us.

Let us offer our lives to the Lord in love
and offer our gifts in works of love for others.

INVITATION TO THE TABLE

The invitation to the table is led from the Communion table.

This is the joyful feast of God's faithfulness,
the abundant banquet of God's steadfast love.

Jesus invites us to this table
not as servants but as friends.
Come with joy.
Come with love.
All is ready.

CHARGE

The blessing and charge may be led from the doors of the church.

Jesus said: If you keep my commandments,
you will abide in my love.
This is my commandment:
that you love one another as I have loved you.
Amen. *or* **Thanks be to God.**

Ascension of the Lord

Acts 1:1–11
Psalm 47 or
 Psalm 93

Ephesians 1:15–23
Luke 24:44–53

OPENING SENTENCES

Clap your hands, all you peoples;
shout to God with loud songs of joy.
For the Lord, the Most High, is awesome,
a great king over all the earth.

Sing praises to God, sing praises;
sing praises to our king, sing praises.
For God is the king of all the earth;
sing praises with a psalm.

PRAYER OF THE DAY

Lord of life, you fill all in all.
We rejoice that in your Son,
heaven has come to earth
and earth is brought to heaven.
Give us a spirit of wisdom and revelation
to look forward in hope
and around us in assurance,
as Jesus leads all creation
into your promised kingdom. **Amen.**

"But you will receive power when the Holy Spirit has come
upon you; and you will be my witnesses in Jerusalem, in all
Judea and Samaria, and to the ends of the earth." When
[Jesus] had said this, as they were watching, he was lifted
up, and a cloud took him out of their sight.

Acts 1:8–9

INVITATION TO DISCIPLESHIP

The invitation to discipleship may be led from the baptismal font.

Jesus ascended into the heavenly places
along with the wounds of the cross
and the dirt of the tomb.

However wounded you may be,
however sullied by the brokenness of this world,
God welcomes you into God's presence,
wrapping you in compassionate arms
and clothing you with the Spirit's power.

Join us in coming to know
the hope to which God calls us
as we bear witness to Christ's power
at work in the world.

PRAYERS OF INTERCESSION

The prayers of intercession may be led from the midst of the congregation.

Holy God, robed in majesty,
send your Spirit upon us as we lift our prayers,
entrusting this world to your power alone.

Send your Spirit upon those who think highly of themselves
and those who think little of themselves.
Bring comfort to those who are vulnerable
and companionship to those who are lonely.
Fill with compassion those who are strong,
and guide them in the way of humility.

Send your Spirit upon those in positions of power
and upon those who feel powerless in this world.
Bring release to those who are held captive
and dignity to those who are oppressed or disregarded.
Fill with wisdom those who hold authority,
and guide them in the way of peace.

Send your Spirit upon those who live in plenty
and upon those who live in need.
Bring security to those who seek refuge,
and satiate those who hunger and thirst.
Fill with hospitality those who know privilege,
and guide them in the way of generosity.

Send your Spirit upon us
and upon all people, O Lord.
Bring faithfulness to all who trust in your grace
and hope to all who look in your reign.
Fulfill the promise of your coming kingdom,
and guide the church by your power from on high.

In the name of Christ,
seated far above all rule and authority,
power and dominion,
and above every name that is named. **Amen.**

INVITATION TO OFFERING

The invitation to offering may be led from the Communion table.

Gifted with the riches of Christ's glorious inheritance,
and clothed with power from on high,
may our lives be an offering of faith in the Lord Jesus,
and our gifts a witness of love toward all people.

INVITATION TO THE TABLE

The invitation to the table is led from the Communion table.

The one who opens minds in understanding
opens heaven to us at this table.
The one who was taken from sight by a cloud
reveals himself in this holy meal.
The one who is seated in the heavenly places
offers himself in bread and wine—gifts of the earth.

The feast of heaven is spread
for us and for all,
by everlasting Love enthroned on high.
So come, let us share in the immeasurable greatness
of the one who cannot be contained
by time or place, flesh or grave.

CHARGE

The blessing and charge may be led from the doors of the church.

The God of our Lord Jesus Christ has clothed you
with a spirit of power and wisdom and revelation.
Go therefore in confidence,
to be Christ's witnesses to the ends of the earth.
Amen. *or* **Thanks be to God.**

Seventh Sunday of Easter

Acts 1:15–17, 21–26   1 John 5:9–13
Psalm 1   John 17:6–19

OPENING SENTENCES

Happy are those who seek God.
God is the sun, the light, and the light maker.

Happy are those who delight in God's Word.
God is the song, the melody, and the song maker.

PRAYER OF THE DAY

God of truth, your words never mislead.
They guide us to life and joy.
Help us to trust you.
Jesus, truth revealing God,
your life of love
brings us into the light of love.
Help us to follow you.
Holy Spirit, God testifying to truth,
you never tire
of teaching us what is important
and how to repent.
Help us to obey. **Amen.**

---

*I write these things to you who believe in the name of the
Son of God, so that you may know that you have eternal life.*

1 John 5:13

INVITATION TO DISCIPLESHIP

The invitation to discipleship may be led from the baptismal font.

Jesus is sending us out
with the same authority and love
as God sent Jesus out.
We are not alone in this world.
This world is not abandoned but embraced.

We are not alone when we speak the truth.
People who speak the truth will also come around us.
People will listen to the truth and leave their lies.

PRAYERS OF INTERCESSION

The prayers of intercession may be led from the midst of the congregation.

Jesus, you have assigned us
the powerful task of intercession:
that whatever we ask in your name,
you will do.
Taking up this awesome task, we pray.

For your church in all nations . . .
that the church would humbly listen to the truth
and courageously stand on the side of the truth,
seeking God's justice for all people.

For the leaders of nations . . .
that they would be seekers of the truth
and not seekers of power,
loving truth instead of lusting for power.

For migrants and refugees,
who do not have a place to call home . . .
that they will find home in your Word
and in this world, and in the fellowship
that gathers to hear your Word.

For this earth and all its inhabitants,
that they may flourish . . .
the rivers that water the trees,
the trees that feed the birds,
the birds that spread the seeds,
that this beautiful dance of mutual service
will continue for all time. **Amen.**

INVITATION TO OFFERING

The invitation to offering may be led from the Communion table.

Did we not receive God's Word freely?
Do we not have the responsibility
to share this free Word of God to as many as possible?
Is not every blessing we have a potential gift to the world?

As a tree does not begrudge its fruits to any,
but lets them fall to the ground and nourish all,
let us release our offerings into God's world.

INVITATION TO THE TABLE

The invitation to the table is led from the Communion table.

We come to the Lord's table
seeking the truth that can free us
from the worst of ourselves.
Here is truth in all her suffering and love.
Jesus, the truth of God's love,
who dies for us but is not overcome by death.

Let this truth be known through all of our lives.
Let it transform us from inside out
into holy and just people of God.

CHARGE

The blessing and charge may be led from the doors of the church.

We know Jesus.
Jesus knows us.
And that is enough for us to keep living
the good life,
the godly life,
the generous life that points people to God.
Amen. *or* **Thanks be to God.**

Day of Pentecost

Acts 2:1–21 *or*
  Ezekiel 37:1–14
Psalm 104:24–34, 35b

Romans 8:22–27 *or*
  Acts 2:1–21
John 15:26–27; 16:4b–15

OPENING SENTENCES

> Amazing God,
> you live in us now as Holy Spirit.
> **We are your holy temple.**
> **Hallelujah!**
>
> We are the community of resurrection
> you have made holy, O God,
> by taking residence among us.
> **We are your holy temple.**
> **Hallelujah!**

PRAYER OF THE DAY

> Creator, you made everything,
> and everything you made
> you looked at and said, "Good."
> Even the Leviathan—"Good."
> And us humans—you said, "Very good."
> Jesus, though we broke your good creation
> by marring God's image,
> you came to restore God's image
> by taking on our brokenness.
> Holy Spirit, you unleashed
> the resurrection power of Jesus
> to restore God's image in us
> and to give us eyes to see God's image
> in people from all cultures and histories.
> We worship you, triune God,
> with all the peoples of the earth. **Amen.**

INVITATION TO DISCIPLESHIP

The invitation to discipleship may be led from the baptismal font.

> Can you believe it?
> God who created all things,
> God who rescued all things,
> now lives in us.
> God wants to make us new
> and renew the creation through us.
>
> That is the gift of discipleship,
> this beautiful responsibility of partnering
> with God's works of creating *shalom*.
>
> It isn't easy,
> but we don't do it alone.
> We are led by the Holy Spirit.
> We only have to follow the Spirit's lead.
> Come join this dance of discipleship.

PRAYERS OF INTERCESSION

The prayers of intercession may be led from the midst of the congregation.

> We are people of resurrection.
> So what we pray, God hears.
> This is the gift of the Spirit:
> our prayers become action in God.
> So in faith we pray.
>
> We lift up the church . . .
> We, the people of God,
> in every corner of the world,
> in local congregations and in the streets,
> pray that we don't diminish the fire of the Spirit,
> that we don't listen to the world's naysayers,
> but that we proclaim Jesus risen and reigning,
> Jesus who breaks prison bars.

We lift up the families of the earth . . .
For those in loneliness,
may they know Emmanuel, God is with us.
For those in oppression,
may they know the Redeemer,
God who lifts up valleys
and flattens haughty mountains.
For those in sin,
may they know the Savior,
God who doesn't leave sinners in sin
but removes them from their addictions
and delivers them into a new day of freedom. **Amen.**

INVITATION TO OFFERING

The invitation to offering may be led from the Communion table.

We have received the gift of God's presence,
the gift of intercession,
the gift of tongues,
and the power to speak the language of love.
These are just a few
of the many gifts of the Holy Spirit
that we have received.

As good stewards of so many gifts,
let us return to God the offerings of our lives.

INVITATION TO THE TABLE

The invitation to the table is led from the Communion table.

The risen Lord invites us to fellowship.
We are being fed, and it is all free.
This is bread that will not leave us hungry.
This is wine that satisfies our soul's deepest longing.
This is a bounteous table.

We come broken and hungry,
but we will be filled with the Holy Spirit.
There will be enough to go around,
so let us invite everyone we know
to join us in this feast.

CHARGE

The blessing and charge may be led from the doors of the church.

As people filled with the Spirit of God,
we have the power of creation at our fingertips.
We have words that can give light or make dark.
So let us speak life.
Our words can bring dry bones back to life.
Once we were broken and brittle, but not anymore.
Love is not impossible.
Nothing is impossible
for us who are brimming with God.
Amen. *or* **Thanks be to God.**

Supplements for the
Narrative Lectionary

Mark 5:1–20

Narrative Lectionary Year 2, 23 (Epiphany 3)
(with Psalm 89:1–4)

See also the resources for the Third Sunday after the Epiphany.

OPENING SENTENCES

O Lord, I will sing of your steadfast love forever;
**I will proclaim your faithfulness
to all generations.**

Your steadfast love is established forever;
your faithfulness is as firm as the heavens.

PRAYER OF THE DAY

Most High God,
you came to us in Jesus Christ
to cast out the power of evil
and deliver us from captivity to death.
Speak to us this day
with your liberating Word,
and fill us with the power
of your life-giving Spirit,
that we may know your mercy
and praise your saving work;
through Christ our Lord. **Amen.**

Then Jesus asked him, "What is your name?"
He replied, "My name is Legion; for we are many."

Mark 5:9

INVITATION TO DISCIPLESHIP

The invitation to discipleship may be led from the baptismal font.

> Jesus seeks to set us free—
> from the shackles that bind us
> and the demons that torment us,
> from the words that hurt us
> and the stories that haunt us.
>
> If you are seeking the healing of Christ
> and the freedom of the Holy Spirit,
> come and join us in the life of faith.
> We welcome you to this community.

PRAYERS OF INTERCESSION

The prayers of intercession may be led from the midst of the congregation.

> God of steadfast love,
> we come before you this day
> lifting up the burdens of our hearts,
> the needs of the church,
> and the suffering of the world.
> Hear our prayer.
>
> For those who are called "unclean" . . .
> embrace them in your love.
>
> For those who are held captive . . .
> liberate them by your grace.
>
> For those who harm themselves . . .
> cover them with your mercy.
>
> For those who cry out for help . . .
> answer them with healing.
>
> For those who struggle with demons . . .
> deliver them from evil.
>
> For those who are outcast . . .
> welcome them in your house.
>
> For those who are afraid . . .
> be their comfort and strength.

God of steadfast love, receive these prayers
and bring about your purpose for all things,
that we may proclaim your faithfulness;
through Jesus Christ our Lord. **Amen.**

INVITATION TO OFFERING

The invitation to offering may be led from the Communion table.

What can we possibly offer in return
for the saving work of God
and the gift of life restored?
Jesus said: Tell everyone
how much the Lord has done for you;
share the good news of God's mercy.

With glad and generous hearts
let us bear witness to God's mercy
through the offering of our lives.

INVITATION TO THE TABLE

The invitation to the table is led from the Communion table.

God has made a covenant with us,
a promise to all generations.
This is the meal of that covenant;
this is the feast of God's steadfast love.

Come to this table.
Come and share in this joyful feast.
In the body and blood of Christ
we will be nourished and strengthened
by the steadfast love of the Lord.

CHARGE

The blessing and charge may be led from the doors of the church.

May you go forth from this place
and tell others of the goodness of God,
the love of Jesus,
and the presence of the Holy Spirit.
Amen. *or* **Thanks be to God.**

Mark 8:14–26

Narrative Lectionary Year 2, 28 (Epiphany 8)
(with Psalm 131)

See also the resources for the Eighth Sunday after the Epiphany.

OPENING SENTENCES

> O Lord, our hearts are humble
> and our eyes are cast down in prayer.
> **We are in the presence of one**
> **too great and marvelous for us.**
>
> Help us to calm and quiet our souls,
> like a weaned child with its mother.
> **You are our hope, O Lord,**
> **from this time on and forevermore.**

PRAYER OF THE DAY

> Loving God,
> through the grace of Jesus Christ
> you provide abundantly for us—
> all that we could ask or imagine.
> Give us the bread we need for this day,
> that we may be nourished to do your will:
> feeding and teaching,
> welcoming and healing,
> all in the name of Christ our Lord. **Amen.**

INVITATION TO DISCIPLESHIP

The invitation to discipleship may be led from the baptismal font.

In this congregation,
we seek to wrestle with the mysteries of our faith,
opening our hearts and minds
to the new way of life God has revealed
in Jesus Christ.

We invite you to join the conversation
and to join this community of faith
as we strive to be faithful followers
of our Savior and Lord.

PRAYERS OF INTERCESSION

The prayers of intercession may be led from the midst of the congregation.

O Lord God, in Jesus Christ you reveal
the extravagance of your grace and love.
Receive our prayers.

Where hearts are hardened,
give new faith to your people.

Where eyes and ears are closed,
reveal the truth that sets us free.

Where there is lack of understanding,
give wisdom and discernment.

Where resources seem scarce,
teach us to share our gifts.

Where people are hungry,
provide abundantly for all.

Where nations are divided,
gather us into your holy realm.

All this we pray in the name of Jesus,
the bread of life. **Amen.**

INVITATION TO OFFERING

The invitation to offering may be led from the Communion table.

In the hands of Jesus,
seven loaves were sufficient
to feed four thousand people,
with seven baskets left over.
In the hands of Jesus,
five loaves were enough
to feed five thousand people,
with twelve baskets left over.

God provides all the gifts we need
to feed a hungry world.
Let us place our lives in Jesus' hands
to see the wonders God will do.

INVITATION TO THE TABLE

The invitation to the table is led from the Communion table.

The table is set with simple things—
a loaf of bread and a cup.
Yet by the grace of God
and the power of the Spirit
it will be an abundant feast
in the body and blood
of Jesus Christ our Lord.

Come, eat and drink
and be filled with the presence of Christ.
Come, taste and see
the goodness of the Lord.

CHARGE

The blessing and charge may be led from the doors of the church.

People of God, let us hope in the Lord
for this time on and forevermore.
Amen. *or* **Thanks be to God.**

Mark 12:1–12 (13–17)

Narrative Lectionary Year 2, 33 (Lent 3)
(with Psalm 86:8–13)

See also the resources for the Third Sunday in Lent.

OPENING SENTENCES

> Teach us your way, O Lord,
> that we may walk in your truth.
> **Give us an undivided heart**
> **to revere your name.**
>
> Let us give thanks to the Lord our God
> with our whole hearts.
> **Let us glorify God's name forever.**

PRAYER OF THE DAY

> Holy God,
> you sent your beloved Son
> to deliver us from sin and death,
> and still we crucified him.
> In your great mercy, forgive us.
> Dismantle systems and structures
> of hatred, greed, and fear,
> and build up your church
> on the chief cornerstone:
> Jesus Christ our Lord. **Amen.**

INVITATION TO DISCIPLESHIP

The invitation to discipleship may be led from the baptismal font.

Are you longing to learn God's way
and walk in the truth of the Lord?

Come with us.
Learn with us.
We are a community of disciples of Jesus,
committed to sharing the steadfast love of the Lord
and giving glory to God in all things.

PRAYERS OF INTERCESSION

The prayers of intercession may be led from the midst of the congregation.

You alone, O Lord,
do great and wondrous things;
you alone are God.
Hear our prayers.

We pray for the church . . .
Build us up as the body of Christ.

We pray for the world . . .
Put an end to violence and greed.

We pray for this community . . .
Protect those who are most vulnerable.

We pray for loved ones . . .
Heal the sick and help the hopeless.

We pray for all in need . . .
Show your mercy to all who suffer.

God of steadfast love,
deliver us from the depths,
that we might rise with gladness
to glorify your name forever;
through Jesus Christ our Lord. **Amen.**

INVITATION TO OFFERING

The invitation to offering may be led from the Communion table.

> By the great mercy of God,
> we have received an inheritance
> that is imperishable, undefiled, and unfading:
> the gift of grace through faith
> in the crucified and risen Lord.
>
> With gratitude for God's amazing grace,
> let us offer our lives and gifts to the Lord.

INVITATION TO THE TABLE

The invitation to the table is led from the Communion table.

> Like wheat gathered in from the field,
> or grapes gathered up from the vineyard,
> God has called the church together
> and has prepared us for a feast.
>
> This is the table of the Lord.
> Come and share in the gifts of God.

CHARGE

The blessing and charge may be led from the doors of the church.

> The stone that the builders rejected
> has become the cornerstone;
> this is the Lord's doing,
> and it is amazing in our eyes!
> Let us go forth to share this good news with all.
> **Amen.** *or* **Thanks be to God.**

John 8:12–30

Narrative Lectionary Year 4, 28 (Epiphany 8)
(with Psalm 36:7–9)

See also the resources for the Eighth Sunday after the Epiphany.

OPENING SENTENCES

How precious is your steadfast love, O God!
All people may take refuge
in the shadow of your wings.

They feast on the abundance of your house,
and you give them drink
from the river of your delights.

For with you, O Lord, is the fountain of life;
in your light we see light.

PRAYER OF THE DAY

Living God,
you sent your only Son
to be the light of the world.
Help us to follow him this day,
that we may not walk in darkness
but have the light of life;
through Jesus Christ our Lord. **Amen.**

INVITATION TO DISCIPLESHIP

The invitation to discipleship may be led from the baptismal font.

In this community of faith,
we seek to testify or bear witness
to the light and love of Jesus Christ.

You are invited to join us on this journey
as we seek to follow the one God sent
to be the light of the world.

PRAYERS OF INTERCESSION

The prayers of intercession may be led from the midst of the congregation.

Gracious God, giver of light and life,
we turn to you in prayer, seeking your will.
Support and strengthen us this day
to accomplish your work in the world.

Help us to testify to the truth
that Jesus is the light of the world.

Lead us on right paths,
that we may know your way of life.

Show us your justice and mercy,
and let us walk humbly with you.

Teach us not to judge others,
lest we ourselves be judged.

Send us forth with food for those who hunger
and drink for those who thirst.

In all things, gracious God,
help us to seek the light of Christ;
in whose holy name we pray. **Amen.**

INVITATION TO OFFERING

The invitation to offering may be led from the Communion table.

How precious is the steadfast love of the Lord:
more precious—and more costly—
than all the treasures of the earth.
For the Lord Jesus Christ gave his life
to deliver us from sin and death forever.

Let us give our lives in his service,
an offering of gratitude for God's grace.

INVITATION TO THE TABLE

The invitation to the table is led from the Communion table.

This is the table of God's steadfast love.
This is a place of refuge for all people.
You are invited to feast
on the abundance of God's house;
to drink deeply
from the river of divine delight.

Come to the table of the Lord.

CHARGE

The blessing and charge may be led from the doors of the church.

Let us go forth in faith, following Jesus,
the light of the world.
Amen. *or* **Thanks be to God.**

Acts 3:1–10

Narrative Lectionary Year 2, 41 (Easter 3)
(with Mark 6:53–56)

See also the resources for the Third Sunday of Easter.

OPENING SENTENCES

> This is the Beautiful Gate of the temple.
> **Now is the hour of prayer.**
>
> Let us go up to the house of the Lord.
> **With awe and wonder,**
> **let us worship God.**

PRAYER OF THE DAY

> Holy God,
> as you worked through Peter
> to heal a vulnerable man
> at the Beautiful Gate of the temple,
> work through us in this place
> to bring healing to the world.
> Fill us with your Spirit,
> that we may rise up with all the earth
> and praise your name in wonder;
> through Jesus Christ our Lord. **Amen.**

> *Peter said, "I have no silver or gold, but what*
> *I have I give you; in the name of Jesus Christ of*
> *Nazareth, stand up and walk."*
>
> *Acts 3:6*

INVITATION TO DISCIPLESHIP

The invitation to discipleship may be led from the baptismal font.

Jesus said: Those who are well
have no need of a physician,
but those who are sick.
I have come to call not the righteous
but sinners to repentance.

Jesus invites us to come as we are,
turning to God in faith, hope, and love.
Come and join the journey of discipleship.

PRAYERS OF INTERCESSION

The prayers of intercession may be led from the midst of the congregation.

Holy and merciful God,
we confess our sinfulness and shortcomings before you.
We have not loved others
as you have loved us . . .
God of grace, **forgive us.**

We have neglected the poor
and those in need . . .
God of grace, **forgive us.**

We have not been faithful stewards
of your creation . . .
God of grace, **forgive us.**

We have not worked for peace and reconciliation
among those who have different beliefs and views . . .
God of grace, **forgive us.**

We have failed to follow you
and have turned to the ways of the world . . .
God of grace, **forgive us.**

O God, cleanse us from our sins.
Renew our hearts and minds
through the Holy Spirit,
that we may serve you;
through Jesus Christ our Lord. **Amen.**

INVITATION TO OFFERING

The invitation to offering may be led from the Communion table.

A man who had never walked
was begging for help
at the temple gate.
Peter said to him:
I have no silver or gold,
but what I have I give you;
in the name of Jesus Christ,
stand up and walk.

Let us give what we have to God,
that we too may work wonders,
contributing to the healing of the world
through the offering of our lives.

INVITATION TO THE TABLE

The invitation to the table is led from the Communion table.

Wherever Jesus went,
people recognized him as a healer.
They rushed toward him,
carrying those unable to walk.
They begged him for help,
only hoping to touch the fringe of his garment,
that they might be healed.

Jesus is here today.
He has prepared a meal for us,
the banquet of his own body and blood,
a feast of healing and grace.
Come, taste and see
the goodness of the Lord.

CHARGE

The blessing and charge may be led from the doors of the church.

Let us arise and praise the Lord,
giving thanks for the grace of God.
Amen. *or* **Thanks be to God.**

Scripture Index

This is an index to the lectionary readings supported in this volume. Revised Common Lectionary readings are listed in regular type; supplemental readings for the Narrative Lectionary are listed in italics.

Contributors

CLAUDIA L. AGUILAR RUBALCAVA, Pastor, First Mennonite Church, Denver

MAMIE BROADHURST, Co-Pastor, University Presbyterian Church, Baton Rouge, Louisiana

DAVID GAMBRELL, Associate for Worship, Office of Theology and Worship, Presbyterian Mission Agency, Presbyterian Church (U.S.A.), Louisville, Kentucky

MARCI AULD GLASS, Pastor and Head of Staff, Calvary Presbyterian Church, San Francisco

MARCUS A. HONG, Director of Field Education and Assistant Professor of Practical Theology, Louisville Presbyterian Theological Seminary, Louisville, Kentucky

KIMBERLY BRACKEN LONG, Liturgical Scholar, Cambridge, Maryland

EMILY McGINLEY, Senior Pastor, City Church, San Francisco

KENDRA L. BUCKWALTER SMITH, Director of the Worship Program, Pittsburgh Theological Seminary, and Associate Pastor for Discipleship, Shadyside Presbyterian Church, Pittsburgh, Pennsylvania

SAMUEL SON, Manager of Diversity and Reconciliation, Executive Director's Office, Presbyterian Mission Agency, Presbyterian Church (U.S.A.), Louisville, Kentucky

SLATS TOOLE, Freelance Writer, Minneapolis

BYRON A. WADE, General Presbyter, Presbytery of Western North Carolina, Morganton, North Carolina

Printed in the USA
CPSIA information can be obtained
at www.ICGtesting.com
LVHW040347140424
777187LV00001B/1